must
SHANGHAI
上海

Yu Garden and Jinmao Tower, ©Oksanaphoto/Dreamstime.com

MICHELIN

General Manager	Cynthia Clayton Ochterbeck

mustsees Shanghai 上海

Editor	Gwen Cannon
Contributing Writers	Florent Bonnefoy, Gwen Cannon, Anne-Marie Scott
Production Manager	Natasha G. George
Cartography	Stéphane Anton, Michèle Cana, Thierry Lemasson
Photo Editor	Yoshimi Kanazawa
Photo Research	Nicole D. Jordan
Researcher	Sean Cannon
Proofreader	Claiborne Linvill
Layout	Nicole D. Jordan
Cover & Interior Design	Chris Bell
Contact Us	Michelin Maps and Guides
	One Parkway South
	Greenville, SC 29615
	USA
	www.michelintravel.com
	Michelin Maps and Guides
	Hannay House
	39 Clarendon Road
	Watford, Herts WD17 1JA
	UK
	☎ (01923) 205 240
	www.ViaMichelin.com
	travelpubsales@uk.michelin.com
Special Sales	For information regarding bulk sales, customized
	editions and premium sales, please contact
	our Customer Service Departments:

USA	1-800-432-6277
UK	(01923) 205 240
Canada	1-800-361-8236

Michelin Apa Publications Ltd

A joint venture between Michelin and Langenscheidt

58 Borough High Street, London SE1 1XF, United Kingdom

© 2010 Michelin Apa Publications Ltd
ISBN 978-1-906261-99-3
Printed: April 2010
Printed and bound: Himmer Winco, China

Note to the reader:

Welcome to Shanghai

Huangpu River and Pudong skyline

p 32

Introduction

**Shanghai:
"City on the Sea"**   **32**

Must See

p 64

p 53

p 84

p 102

TABLE OF CONTENTS

★★★ ATTRACTIONS

Unmissable historic, cultural and natural sights.

Shanghai Museum   p 40, p 69

Suzhou   p 111

© Mikhail Nekrasov/Dreamstime.com

Nanjing Lu   p 40

People's Square   p 40

The Bund   p 34

Lingyin Temple, Hangzhou   p 108

West Lake, Hangzhou   p 102

Dragon Boat Racing   p 75

Shopping   p 88

David Shen Kai/Apa Publications

Longwu Kung Fu Center
p 78, p 82

Javem Ran/Longwu International Kung Fu Center

Traditional Chinese Opera   p 84

MUST KNOW

Tai chi p 65

Bicycling p 74

Courtesy Shanghai Ocean Aquarium

Shanghai Ocean Aquarium p 80

Shanghai Zoo p 57, p 81

★★★ ATTRACTIONS

Unmissable historic, cultural and natural sights

For more than 75 years, people have used Michelin stars to take the guesswork out of travel. Our star-rating system helps you make the best decision on where to go, what to do, and what to see.

★★★	Unmissable
★★	Worth a trip
★	Worth a detour
No star	Recommended

MUST KNOW

ACTIVITIES

Unmissable activities, entertainment, restaurants and hotels
For every historic and natural sight in Shanghai there are many more activities. We recommend all of the activities in this guide, but our top picks are highlighted with the Michelin Man logo.

STAR ATTRACTIONS

IDEAS AND TOURS

Throughout this thematic guide you will find inspiration for many different ways to experience Shanghai. The following is a selection of ideas to start you off. The sights in **bold** are found in the index.

WALKING TOURS

Shanghai is a great place to wander around, be it the malls, the riverbanks or the city parks (just be aware of the possibility of pickpockets). *The following self-guided walking tours are tailored to the sights found in DISTRICTS.*

The Bund★★★

Heritage projects are ensuring the Bund retains its handsome 1920 and 30s architecture. This historic heart of the city's financial and commercial firms is a place to see Art Deco- and colonial-style buildings lining the **promenade★★★** along the Huangpu River, as well as to shop and dine. Begin with the **People's Heroes Memorial** in **Huangpu Park** and continue south, paralleling Zhongshan Dong Lu. Pass the **Bank of China★★**, the **Customs House★** and other grand buildings to end at the **Bund Museum**.

People's Square and Nanjing Lu★★★

This massive public space and major shopping street are usually crowded with people. This walk provides an introduction to some of the major sights of the area. Start at the No. 1 Department Store at 800 **Nanjing Dong Lu** and walk west, crossing Xizang Zhong Lu, and passing the **Park Hotel★★** on your right. Continue west along the northern edge of **People's Park** and turn left onto Huangpo Bei Lu, at the corner where the **Shanghai Art Museum** sits. On your right rises **Tomorrow Square**, and farther down on your left, you can't miss the futuristic-looking **Grand Theatre**. Turn left onto People's Dajie Lu (People's Avenue) to stroll this grand boulevard that runs along the southern part of People's Park, where the **Shanghai Museum★★★** resides.

Architecture on the Bund

MUST KNOW

Pudong skyline

Former French Concession★★

South of People's Square lie the charming, tree-shaded streets of the old French Concession. It may be best to begin at the **Arts and Crafts Museum** at the corner of Fuxing Xi Lu and Fenyang Lu. Move east along Fuxing Xi Lu to see the **Ruijin Hotel★**, before turning left onto Maoming Nan Lu, home to trendy shops and cafes. You will come to the **Jin Jiang Hotel★★**, and opposite, the **Former French Sports Club★**. Across Changle Lu sits the 1931 **Lyceum Theatre**. Go east to Shimen Yi Lu and turn right to head south to Fuxing Zhong Lu. Turn left onto it to reach **Fuxing Park★** and **Sun Yat-sen's Residence★★**.

Old Town★★

Home of **Yu Garden★★**, the old part of Shanghai also plays host to temples, markets and mosques. Begin at the **Confucius Temple★** on Wenmaio Lu. Walk east to Zhuangjia Jie and turn left to reach Fuxing Dong Lu. Head east *(right)* to Ziaotaoyuan Jie to see the

Mosque of the Small Peaches Garden★. Continue on Fuxing Dong Lu and turn left onto Henan Nan Lu, walking north until you reach Fuyou Lu. Take a right and you'll see the **Fuyou Lu Mosque**. Then turn right onto Houjia Lu and continue south to end your walk at Fang Bang Zhong Lu Flea Market.

The Pudong★★

This "city" of towering skyscrapers on the east side of the Huangpu River may be somewhat intimidating to those on foot. But the walk along the river offers splendid views of both the Pudong's iconic high rises as well as the Bund's buildings on the other side. Start at the south end of the grand boulevard known as Binjiang Dadao, where the ferry from the Bund disembarks. Then head north along the river to the **Pearl of the Orient Tower★**. As you walk, look to your right and you'll see the **Jinmao Tower★★** and the **World Financial Center★★** in the background.

Xujiahui
See Walking Tour p56.

13

RIVER TOURS

The city's backbone, the **Huangpu River** has always played a key role in the lives of the Shanghainese: it opened Shanghai to the rest of China and to the world. Its route was honed over three centuries (12–15C) by the hands of men; its downstream waters were diverted from the sea so the river would be directly linked to the **Yangtze River** and its vast fertile basin. In the middle of the 19C, the first Westerners established businesses on its banks, combining their offices with a warehouse and their place of residence.

The people of Shanghai gave a name to each side of the river bank: **Puxi**, or "West of the Huangpu," is the historic cradle of the city; the **Pudong** is "East of the Huangpu." This gigantic fluvial artery carries all manner of boats: ferries heading to Japan or Korea, cruise ships coming back from the Yangtze River, battleships at the dockside, tour boats and other ships moored in the middle of the river, and the well-known overloaded barges linked one to another.

You can appreciate the river (and the city as well) from a waterside perspective by taking a **cruise★★** on the Huangpu River. One hour-, 2 hour- and 3.5-hour cruises are available from the Bund. One of the most popular companies offering river tours is the **Shanghai Huangpu River Cruise Company** (021 54106831; www.pjrivercruise. com) or ask your hotel to make reservations for you. *For details on river tours, see FOR FUN.*

SHANGHAI'S NATURE

Though sizable natural settings are getting more difficult to find in Shanghai, a bird's eye view of the city reveals a number of protected green spaces in the form of parks and gardens. In the central part of the city, **People's Park** has two vast expanses of greenery that are perfect for strolling and **people-watching**. In the Pudong, the riverside promenade called **Binjiang Dadao** as well as **Century Park**, with its large lake, offer plenty of breathing space. More intimate spots include **Fuxing Park★** in the Former French Concession and **Mengqing Park**, edging Suzhou

River cruise on the Huangpu

Creek. The **Botanical Garden**★ occupies a very spacious 197-plus acres in the Xujiahui section of Shanghai. Visit one or all, as your time permits. *For descriptions of the above, see PARKS AND GARDENS.*

SIDE TRIPS

Several side trips from Shanghai offer opportunities to experience daily life and sights in nearby Chinese towns, although it is best to allow two or three days for these excursions rather than try to pack them into just one (hectic) day. Except for Putuoshan *(accessible by ferry from Shanghai)*, the following destinations are reachable by train, bus and car. The small island of **Putuoshan**★★, south of Shanghai in the Zhoushan Archipelago, has mountains sacred to Buddhists, sandy beaches and several fine temples. The unique city of **Hangzhou**★★★, southwest of Shanghai, is famed for its serene lake backdropped by verdant hills. Due west of Shanghai sits the historic city of **Suzhou**★★★, celebrated for its many classical gardens, designated as UNESCO World Heritage Sites. The city's most recent attraction is the spectacular **Suzhou Museum**★★★, designed by renowned Chinese architect I.M. Pei. Just southeast of Suzhou lie the picturesque villages of **Tongli**★★ and **Zhouzhuang**★★, threaded with bridges and canals bordered by ancient dwellings. *For detailed descriptions of the above destinations, as well as a listing of recommended places to stay overnight and to dine, see the specific entry in the Table of Contents or find it in the Index at the back of the guide.*

Quick Trips
Stuck for ideas? Try these:

IDEAS AND TOURS

15

CALENDAR OF EVENTS

Listed below is a selection of Shanghai's most popular annual events (dates and times vary since many events are based on the Chinese lunar calendar; check in advance). For details call, or access online, Shanghai Municipal Tourism Administration: (021) 962020 or www.meet-in-shanghai.net. See p62 for some of the city's religious festivals.

JANUARY/FEBRUARY

Chinese New Year

The pinnacle of Chinese holidays, this celebration, occurring sometimes in January, is officially three days, but the buildup and aftermath can prolong it to two weeks. Festivities and family reunions are held in temples, parks, homes and restaurants. Gifts are taken to family members and *hongbaos* (red packets of money) are given to the children. Fireworks ring out the old year and welcome the new, and dumplings are eaten for good luck.

Lantern Festival

Held 15 days after the Chinese New Year, this festival is celebrated with displays of paper lanterns in shops, temples and parks; consumption of sweet rice balls; dancing; and fireworks. Yu Garden's bazaar has crafts for the occasion. The Temple of the City God is especially colorful during the festival.

MARCH

Birthday of Guanyin

This religious festival is celebrated in the city's Buddhist temples to honor the goddess of Mercy.

Shanghai Peach Blossom Festival

Held over a three-week period beginning late March, this annual event glorifies the peach, Chinese symbol of longevity. It centers in the town of Huinan in the Nanhui suburb of Shanghai, specifically at the Chengbei Folk Peach Orchard, with its acres of peaches *(021 58000521; www.shanghai.gov.cn)*.

February: *Lantern Festival at the Temple of the City God*

APRIL

Qing Ming Jie

Many Chinese visit temples on this public holiday to clean the tombs of their deceased ancestors. The Chinese temples are busy with people armed with brooms to sweep the graves clean and pay their respects to their ancestors.

Longhua Temple Fair

For two weeks in April, the Longhua Temple *(see PLACES OF WORSHIP)* is the site of Buddhist ceremonies as well as Chinese opera, a parade and other celebratory activities.

Formula 1 Chinese Grand Prix

This exciting motor sports event in mid-April *(see FOR FUN)* takes place at the Shanghai International Circuit *(www.icsh.sh.cn)*.

Shanghai International Tea Culture Festival

This 10-day festival attracts tea lovers from around the world to Shanghai's Zhabei district for tea ceremonies and seminars *(www.tea-sh.cn)*.

MAY

World Dragon and Lion Dance Championship

This traditional sport originated in ancient China some 2,000 years ago. Today more than 50 teams from some 30 countries participate in the colorful spectacle, in which a team of athletes maneuvers a 25ft or longer dragon by metal rods attached to it.

The dragon can be made of paper, cloth, grass or other materials. The Yuanshen Sports Centre in Pudong New Area was the 2009 Shanghai venue for the event

(http://dragonlion.sport.org.cn or www.dragon-lion.org).

Dragon Boat Festival

This national holiday takes place in late May or early June. In Shanghai, teams of rowers race to the beat of drums in fancifully decorated boats on Suzhou Creek. The colorful competition is based on the legend of Qu Yuan, who lived more than 2,000 years ago *(see FOR FUN)*.

Shanghai Spring International Music Festival

Renowned musicians and international orchestras perform at this two-week event at the Shanghai Oriental Art Centre in May *(425 Dingxiang Lu, Pudong; 021 38424800; www.shoac.com.cn)*.

JUNE

Shanghai International Film Festival

Considered the only top-drawer film festival in all of Asia, this event lasts one week in mid-June. Film stars from various countries make grand entrances on the red carpet, and juried prizes are awarded for various categories. Check in advance if the Chinese films you want to see have English subtitles *(021 62537115; www.siff.com)*.

Shanghai TV Festival

This five-day event is held annually at the Shanghai Exhibition Centre. The public is invited *(ticket must be purchased)* to see the latest in TV technology, meet local TV personalities and purchase merchandise at sponsored booths. *(021) 62808991; www.stvf.com)*.

May: World Dragon and Lion Dance Championship

Tanakawho/Flickr.com

JULY
Anniversary of the Chinese Communist Party
Based at the Site of the CCP Inaugural Meeting *(see DISTRICTS)*, this July 1 celebration of the party's founding includes a concert at the Shanghai Oriental Art Centre and various municipal ceremonies *(374 Huangpi Nan Lu; 021 53832171)*.

SEPTEMBER
Shanghai Tourism Festival
From the third Saturday in September to mid-October, the city spotlights its tourist attractions, culture and history. Past events have included a parade with floats, musical entertainment, bazaars, festivities at Yu Garden and fireworks in Century Park *(021 23115561; www.tourfest.org)*.

Mooncake Festival
With feasts, dancing, moon-gazing, and pastries called mooncakes, this festival, also called **Mid-Autumn Festival**, takes place usually in mid-September or early October. It commemorates the 14C uprising against the Mongols during China's Yuan dynasty, when rebels hid their plans for revolt on pieces of paper in mooncakes. Market stalls sell the special cakes, which are filled with lotus paste and a salty yolk in the center, symbolizing the moon. Yu Garden is decorated for the occasion.

Shanghai Biennale
Held every two years at the **Shanghai Art Museum** since 1996, this themed exhibit invites participation from Chinese artists and artists from around the world to showcase their contemporary works to the public. In 2010 the show will take place from September through November *(325 Nanjing Xi Lu; 021 63272829; www.shanghaibiennale.org)*.

OCTOBER
National Day
October 1 is the date in 1949 that Mao Zedong declared the country the People's Republic of China. Its creation is memorialized every year with fireworks, Chinese flags and a week-long holiday.

International Arts Festival
This month-long tribute to the arts showcases 150 performances at various venues throughout Shanghai. Chinese operas, symphony orchestra concerts, modern dance, acrobatic shows, magic acts, theatrical productions and music competitions fill the city from mid-October through mid-November *(www.artsbird.com)*.

JZ Music Festival Shanghai
This two-day event in mid-October is reputedly the largest outdoor music fest in Shanghai. Concert-goers sit on the grass at **Century Park** to enjoy

performances by international musicians. A well-known jazz artist headlines the opening ceremony at a local theater. Free concerts are usually staged in People's Square and other public spaces a few days before the festival *(021 64317113; www.jzfestival.com)*.

Shanghai Fashion Week

Every spring (March and April) for the past 15 years, Shanghai has flaunted its couture at various events and venues in the city. Fall collections are paraded at a second Fashion Week in autumn: in October 2009, for example, designer shows were hosted by the Grand Central Hotel Shanghai. The annual **Shanghai International Fashion Cultural Festival** is a municipal government-sponsored event held at the same time to boost the city's fashion industry. Past designers attending have included Ungaro, Gautier, Sonia Rykiel, and Vivienne Westwood *(www.sifc.org.cn)*.

China Shanghai International Piano Competition

This 10-day competition—going into its sixth year—is held in concert halls at the Shanghai Oriental Art Centre and the Conservatory of Music *(see PERFORMING ARTS)*. For lovers of piano music, there are plenty of opportunities to hear Beethoven and other masters *(021 64689585; www.csipc.org)*.

NOVEMBER

International Magic Festival & Competition

For six years in early November, magicians (usually a dozen) from all over the world have thrilled audiences with their prestidigitation at this annual contest. The venue for the gala opening show and competition is the main hall of the Shanghai International Gymnastics Center *(www.shigc.com)* near Zhongshan Xi Lu *(021 66523097; www.shanghaimagic.cn)*.

International Puppet Festival & Competition

November 2009 was the premiere of this five-day festival, held at the **Shanghai Puppet Theatre**. The theater can accommodate an audience upwards of 200 people, and stages productions such as *Cinderella* and *The Little Mermaid* throughout the year. At the festival, a dozen puppeteers from various countries were chosen to compete for government-supplied prizes *(Fifth floor, 388 Nanjing Xi Lu; 021 63345208)*.

Shanghai International Marathon

Sponsored by China's Toray Industries in recent years, this marathon attracts thousands of contestants despite Shanghai's poor air quality. The course starts at Century Plaza on Nanjing Dong Lu and moves west along heavily trafficked streets lined with enthusiastic crowds to the outskirts of the city *(www.shmarathon.com)*.

DECEMBER

Christmas Day

Christmas in Shanghai is not officially recognized, but festivities and gatherings take place largely among expatriates, and even some of the younger Chinese residents. Area Christian churches hold special services, and the city's commercial establishments decorate their shops and stores.

WHEN TO GO

Shanghai's **climate** is subtropical and influenced by its proximity to the sea. Its four seasons are distinct. Lasting only about two months each, spring and autumn are definitely the best seasons to visit, since temperatures are mild and rainfall is minimal. From March to May, Shanghai's weather is generally pleasant. Average **spring** temperatures hover in the mid-60s in April and mid-70s in May. The **summer** months (Jun–Sept) bring hot, very humid conditions, when clouds cover the sky and dense smog hangs over the metropolis. Bottled **drinking water** is a must here, since the heat and humidity can quickly lead to dehydration. Visitors unaccustomed to these humid conditions may find themselves quickly tired. If you visit in summer, consider taking a trip to nearby **Putuoshan Island**, with its sandy beaches and warm waters. In June and July **monsoon rains** are likely; almost 60 percent of the city's annual rainfall of 50 inches occurs during the flood season, which may last from June to September. **Winter** months can be cold, but snow is rare. In fact, Shanghai typically enjoys 230 days a year that are free of frost. Temperatures in January and February can fall below freezing, but usually they last only a few days.

If you plan your visit to coincide with one of Shanghai's **festivals**, accommodations should be booked far in advance, especially for the Chinese New Year *(see CALENDAR OF EVENTS)*.

The best clothes to wear in the summer are light cottons. Bring a light coat for spring and fall, and a heavy coat for winter. An umbrella is always useful; it can double as a parasol, a popular accessory among Shanghainese.

KNOW BEFORE YOU GO
Useful Websites

www.meet-in-shanghai.net – The Shanghai Municipal Tourism Administration's informative, comprehensive site.

www.shanghai.gov.cn – The official website of the Shanghai municipal government.

www.shanghaidaily.com – This local newspaper, published in English, features events, entertainment, restaurants and sports.

www.cityweekend.com. cn/shanghai – This online version, in English, of the free publication *City Weekend* focuses on cultural events, parties, restaurants, bars.

www.smartshanghai.com – This website targets Shanghai's expatriate community and features theater and restaurant reviews, nightlife and the art scene.

Average Seasonal Temperatures in Shanghai				
	Jan	**Apr**	**Jul**	**Oct**
Avg. High	8°C/46°F	19°C/66°F	32°C/90°F	23°C/73°F
Avg. Low	1°C/34°F	10°C/50°F	23°C/73°F	14°C/57°F

Tourism Offices

www.meet-in-shanghai.net – Prior to arrival, it's best to access the website of Shanghai Municipal Tourism Administration (SMTA).

Visitor Centers in Shanghai – SMTA offices are located at:

◆ 561 Nanjing Dong Lu. (8621) 63503718.

◆ 303 Moling Lu, at the south exit of the Shanghai Railway Station. (8621) 63539920.

Tourist **information kiosks** are located at both the Hongqiao and Pudong airports.

SMTA Tourist Hotline – 962020 (in Shanghai), or (8621) 962020 (Overseas).

The following **English-language publications** are available at hotels and bars: *That's Shanghai, City Weekend* and *Shanghai Talk*. You'll find information on new and happening places in Shanghai, plus news, practical information, show times and helpful articles on Chinese culture.

International Visitors

Foreign Embassies in Shanghai

American Consulate – 1038 West Nanjing Road, Westgate Mall, 8th floor. (8621) 32174650 (business hours); emergency after-hours (8621) 64333936. http://shanghai.usembassy-china.org.cn. Open Mon–Fri 8am–11:30am & 1:30pm–3:30pm (closed Tue afternoons).

Canadian Consulate – Room 604 West Tower, Shanghai Centre, 1376 West Nanjing Road. (8621) 32792800; after-hours emergency contact information (Canadian citizens only) 10-800-140-0125. www.shanghai.gc.ca. Open Mon–Fri 1pm–4:30pm.

Entry Requirements

The following information is subject to change. Check with official sources for updates at the time you plan to travel to China.

Citizens of the US and Canada must have a **visa** issued by the People's Republic of China, in addition to a **passport** with an expiration date not less than six months after your planned departure from China. Tourist visas, valid for three months from the issue date, permit travel within China for a maximum of 60 days (extensions to 90 days are possible from within China for an additional 100 yuans).

US Visa Office of the China Embassy: 2201 Wisconsin Ave., NW, Suite 110, Washington, DC 20007. 202-338-6688. www.china-embassy.org.

For a full explanation of the entry and visa requirements for Shanghai, go to: www.meet-in-shanghai.net/visa.php.

Shanghai Customs

Before arriving in China, you must fill out a **baggage declaration** form. Cameras and photographic equipment are allowed for non-professional photography only. In any event, it's becoming rarer for visitors to be stopped at the border. Note that it is against the law to transport any object more than 100 years old outside China (keep receipts and business card of merchants for purchases you make in China to present to customs, upon request). For more information regarding customs regulations, visit **http://shanghai.customs.gov.cn**. For customs upon reentry to the US, access www.cbp.gov. Goods **prohibited** from being brought into Shanghai (and China in general) include: arms and ammunition, printed and electronic matter (CDs, tapes, etc.) considered detrimental to China's interests, addictive drugs, fruits, and animal products *(for pets, see below)*. Cigars, cigarettes and alcohol above a designated amount are among items brought into Shanghai for which **duties** must be paid. *Before you depart for Shanghai, be sure to see the full listings of prohibited, dutiable and controlled items online at http://shanghai.customs.gov.cn/Default.aspx?tabid=5674.*

Travelers with Pets

It's almost impossible to bring a domesticated animal into China. Owners are required to provide an international **health certificate** issued 24 hours prior to departure from the home country, in addition to updated proof of vaccination (especially against rabies). Animals accompanying non-residents must be quarantined in isolation for a period of 30 days upon arrival.

Health

Before You Go – It is strongly recommended that, before departure, US citizens check http://travel.state.gov for any travel advisories regarding China.

Illnesses – It's not uncommon to experience digestive difficulties when traveling in China. Unfamiliar cooking methods, food products and highly spiced regional dishes can often bring on intestinal distress. To reduce the likelihood of problems, drink only **bottled water**, avoid ice, and be sure to wash all fruits and vegetables thoroughly in bottled water before consuming them.

Visitors are urged to take the following precautions against **avian flu**: avoid all contact with fowl and birds; avoid visiting poultry farms and poultry markets; do not consume raw or lightly cooked foods, especially meats and eggs; wash hands frequently with soap and hot water; and avoid drinking tap water; drink only bottled water.

Be aware of **HIV/AIDS** and take steps to protect yourself.

First-aid kits – Be sure to bring a first-aid kit on your trip. Your kit should include the following: aspirin or other analgesic medicine; anti-diarrhea medicine; sunscreen; bandages; antibacterial ointment and insect repellant to ward off mosquitoes and other insects.

Sanitation – Do not drink tap water or have ice. Wash fruits and vegetables thoroughly.

Medical Facilities – Shanghai has medical centers capable of addressing basic and serious medical problems. More complicated situations should be handled back in your home country. Contact the reception desk at your hotel or any major hotel for help in communicating clearly with doctors.

Doctors – Most doctors practice traditional (rather than Western) medicine. Your embassy or consulate may be able to provide you with a list and contact information of doctors available for consultation with American travelers.

Ambulance – Dial 120 for an ambulance.

Hospitals – The US Consulate website has a list of clinics and medical facilities. Also check

http://shanghai.usembassy-china.org.cn/medical_facilities.html.
Ruijin Hospital: (8621) 64370045. www.rjh.com.cn. Shanghai's main hospital; English-speaking doctors.
Huashan Hospital Foreigners Clinic: 12 Wulumuqi Zhong Road, off Huashan Road, in the Former French Concession, (8621) 52889998 or 62483986, www.sh-hwmc.com.cn. Open 8am–10pm (emergency 24 hrs/day). Note the fees at this clinic may be very expensive.

Immunization
Although no **vaccinations** are required to enter China, visitors should check that all routine immunizations (including tetanus) are up to date. Vaccinations against typhoid fever, hepatitis A and B, and meningococcal disease are also strongly recommended. Health authorities advise that visitors should have the recommended inoculations before arriving in Shanghai. For more information on travel to China, check with the Centers for Disease Control website, www.cdc.gov/travel.

Special Considerations
Women Traveling Alone – It's safe to travel unescorted in China; women alone here don't encounter the harassment typical of some tourist destinations. Nonetheless, it's a good idea to avoid venturing out on foot late at night.
Traveling as a Couple – Chinese couples are very modest about displaying affection in public. Nevertheless the Chinese are quite tolerant of foreign visitors when it comes to affectionate behavior (within reason).

Older Travelers – The Chinese readily give their seats to older travelers on public transportation. You'll find up escalators in all metro stations, and elevators in commercial buildings and most hotels.
Gifts – In almost any situation, the Chinese are ready to lend a helping hand to a traveler. It's a good idea to carry something small from your home country to offer as a token of thanks. Such a gesture is appreciated, although it's customary in China to refuse a gift at first.

GETTING THERE
If your plans call for air travel within China, make be sure to reserve tickets well in advance, especially during tourist seasons. Only three Chinese airlines allow you to make reservations from outside the country: Air China, China Eastern and China Southern. For other airlines, you must make reservations from within China. The following websites provide rail and airline schedule information for travel within China:
Flights: www.travelchinaguide.com/china-flights/index.htm.
Trains: www.travelchinaguide.com/china-trains/index.htm.

By Air
Shanghai has two major airports, Hongqiao and Pudong:
Hongqiao Airport – *(8621) 52604620. www.shairport.com.* Smaller and closer (9mi west of downtown central Shanghai), Hongqiao Airport serves several domestic airlines.
Baggage storage – located in the domestic arrivals hall. 110 yuans/day, 30 yuans/3hrs.

23

Pudong Airport – *(8621) 96990. www.shairport.com*. Located 19mi east of downtown, Shanghai's main international airport was designed by French architect Paul Andreu. Pudong handles all international air traffic and most domestic flights.

Baggage storage is available from 6am until the arrival of the last flight of the day. 100 yuans/day, 30 yuans/3hrs.

Lost Luggage – Office is located in the domestic arrivals terminal, between gates 8 and 9. (8621) 68346324.

Airlines – A number of airlines serve Pudong, including the following:

Air Canada
Room 3901, United Plaza, 1468 Nanjing Rd. 400 811 2001. www.aircanada.cn

Air China
307 Jiali Center, 1515 Nanjing West Rd., Shanghai. 8:30am–6pm. 4008-100-999. www.airchina.com.cn

China Eastern Airlines
258 Weihai Rd. (8621) 95808, or 888-359-5108 (North America). www.flychinaeastern.com

Dragonair
138 Huaihai Zhong Rd., Shanghai Square Office Tower, 21st floor 9am–5pm. 400-888-6628 or (8620) 83882498 (international). www.dragonair.com

Northwest/KLM Airlines
Suite 1007, Kerry Centre No. 1515 Nanjing Rd. 400-814-0081 or (international). www.nwa.com

Shanghai Airlines
212 Jiangning Rd. 8:30am–5:30pm (8621) 62558888. www.shanghai-air.com

United Airlines
Room 14-305, International Departure Terminal. (8621) 133114567 or 800-810-8282 (toll-free China). www.cn.united.com.

Airport Transfers
From Pudong Airport:
Taxi – Service to downtown Shanghai takes about an hour or more from Pudong, depending on traffic, and costs around 160 yuans.

Train – The high-speed **Maglev** Train links Pudong Airport with the Longyang Road metro station in 7min; departs every 15min daily 7am–9pm. 50 yuans one-way.

Bus – The bus remains the most practical and least expensive (2–30 yuans) way to travel between the Pudong Airport and Shanghai. Bus lines include:

Line 1: between Pudong and Hongqiao Airport. 7am–11pm, every 15–25min. Night service by way of Longyang Road metro station after 11pm. 30 yuans.

Line 2: between Pudong and the Jing'an Temple. 7am–11pm every 15–25min, 19 yuans.

Pudong International Airport
© Stephan Thiel/Fotolia.com

Line 3: between Pudong and the Galaxy Hotel by way of Xu Jia Hui and the Longyang Road metro station. 7am–11pm, every 15–20min, 2–20 yuans.

Line 4: between Pudong and Hongkou Stadium. 7am–11pm, every 20min, 2–18 yuans.

Line 5: between Pudong and the Shanghai Railway Station. 7am–11pm, every 20min, 2–18 yuans.

Line 6: between Pudong and Zhongshan Park. 7am–11pm, every 20–30min, 2–20 yuans.

Line 7: between Pudong and the Shanghai South Railway Station. 7:50am–11am, every 30min, 20 yuans.

Line 8: between Pudong and Guzong Road, Hucheng Huan Road. 8am–6pm every 2hrs, 2–16 yuans.

From Hongqiao Airport:

Taxi – By taxi, it takes between 20–30min to get to central Shanghai from Hongqiao. 50 yuans.

Bus – Several bus lines connect Hongqiao Airport with downtown. (8621) 52604620 (information line for Hongqiao Airport):

Special Line: direct to Jing'an Temple. 7:50am–last arrival, every 15–25min, 4 yuans.

Line 938: between Hongqiao and Yangjiadu (Pudong), 6am–midnight every 8–15min, 2–7 yuans.

Line 925A: between Hongqiao and People's Square, 6am–11pm, every 10min, 2–4 yuans.

Line 941: between Hongqiao and the Shanghai Railway Station, 6:30am–11pm, every 10–12min, 2–4 yuans.

Line 1: between Hongqiao and Pudong Airport, 6am–11pm, every 15–25min, 30 yuans.

Line 806: between Hongqiao and Lupu Bridge, 6am–11pm, every 10–15min, 2–5 yuans.

Line 807: between Hongqiao and Qingjian New Estate, 6am–11pm, every 20min, 1–2.5 yuans.

GETTING AROUND
By Bicycle

Except for the city's major arteries, which are heavily trafficked, biking is a practical way to explore Shanghai, especially quiet areas such as Old Town and the Former French Concession. It pays to be vigilant elsewhere, as traffic moves quickly and often unpredictably. Bicycles can be rented from **Giant Bicycle Store**, 743 Jianguo Xi Lu, off Hengshan Lu, Xujiahui. (8621) 6437 5041. www.shanghaicycling. com. 9am–8pm *(see also FOR FUN)*.

By Bus

Buses are an economical way to get around (1–2 yuans), but are often very crowded, delayed by traffic, and challenging for travelers who don't speak Chinese. Visitors may find it easier to navigate Shanghai by metro or taxi.

There are several interurban bus stations in Shanghai. It costs about the same (and takes about the same amount of time) to travel between cities by bus or train.

Hengfeng Lu Bus Station – In front of Hanzhong Road metro station. (8621) 63173912 or 56630230. Service to Hangzhou, Suzhou, Nanking, Shaoxing, Ningbo. Freeway bus service to Bejing (13 hrs).

West Bus Station (Xujiahui Station) – 211 Hongqiao Rd. (8621) 64697356. Service to Hangzhou, Suzhou, Nanking, Shaoxing, Ningbo, Yagshou and Wuxi.

Transportation Touring Tip

If you intend to stay in Shanghai for several days, the **Shanghai Public Transportation Card** or *jiaotong* is a convenient way to pay for public transportation around the city. This reloadable fare card is accepted for all forms of public transportation within the city of Shanghai (including buses, metros, ferries and taxis). The card itself is free of charge (there is a refundable deposit of 20 yuans); you can load it with any amount of credit you wish. For details, access www.sptcc.com.

Hutai Lu and Zhongshan Bei Lu Bus Stations – Service to Shanghai and nearby areas, especially Suzhou and Hangzhou.
Shanghai Stadium Bus Station – 666 Shilong Lu. (8621) 54353535. www.ctnz.net (Chinese only).

By Car

To drive in China, a **Chinese driver's license** is required; international driver's licenses are not valid. Only residents may obtain a Chinese license. Tourists, however, can rent a car with a driver from a car rental agency (600–800 yuans/day), or negotiate a daily rate with a taxi driver (around 300-600 yuans or higher). Some hotels have chauffeured cars for rent. The **Chinese International Travel Service** (CITS) is another source for car rentals: 1001 Changan Road, No. 1, Building 16. (8621) 54106838. www.nscits.com.

By Ship

Shangai is one of the world's busiest sea ports.
Ferries – Ferries on the Huangpu River shuttle passengers between the Bund and Pudong *(see text box in DISTRICTS)*.
Shiliupu Pier – 111 Zhongshan Dong Er Rd., on the Bund. Daily service to Putuoshan. Trips up the Yangtze River via Nantong, Nanking, Wuhu, Guichi, Jiujiang and Wuhan. Boat travel is an economical and original way to experience Shanghai and the surrounding area.
International Passenger Terminal – Dongdaming Rd. (021) 65452288. Service to Hong Kong and international destinations.
Victoria Cruises – This American company offers excursions along the Yangtze River, including superb 9-day cruises between Shanghai and Chongqing. Prices start at $1,470. www.victoriacruises.com.

By Taxi

Taxis are the most practical way to travel in Shanghai. They are easy to flag (except on weekend evenings, in rainy weather or in traffic jams) and are reasonably priced: trips within the downtown area generally cost about 15–20 yuans.

On Waibaidu Bridge

David Shen Kai/Apa Publications

The price is determined by the number of miles traveled and by the type of vehicle (there are three vehicle categories defined by level of comfort, with slightly different rates). **Day rates** (5am–11pm): 12 yuans for the first 3km; 2.40 yuans/km for the next 3–10km; and 3.20 yuans/km after 10km. **Nighttime rates** (11pm–5am): 16 yuans for the first 3km, then 2.70 yuans/km for the next 3–10km; then 4.10 yuans/km after 10km. To avoid being overcharged, make certain that the driver does not activate the rate counter until the journey has begun. Taxi drivers rarely speak English; to communicate your destination, have the address written in Mandarin or use a cell phone to have someone at your destination tell the driver where you want to go. Also keep the business card of your hotel to show the taxi driver for return trips. Check the taxi when you exit to be sure you've taken all your belongings, and always keep your receipt.

Bashi Taxi: (021) 96840.
Dazhong Taxi: (021) 96822. www.96822.com.
Jinjiang Taxi: (021) 96961. www.96961.net.

By Train

The rail services in Shanghai:
Shanghai Rail Station– 303 Moling Rd., Zhabei. (8621) 63179090. Trains for Bejing, Suzhou and Hong Kong depart from the main railway station, located north of downtown. Express trains depart for Bejing (14 hours) at 6pm and 10pm.
Shanghai South Rail Station – 289 Old Humin Rd. Xuhui District. (8621) 51105110. Service to Hangzhou and nearby areas. Information: (8621) 63179090 or 95105123; reservations (toll-free) 800-820-7890.
Beijing-Shanghai High-Speed Railway – When completed, it will reduce the 809mi journey to only 4hrs (departs from Hongqiao).

Shanghai metro

27

On Foot

There are pleasant places to walk even in such a big city as Shanghai. Promenades along both sides of the Huangpu River are designed for pedestrians. Tree-line streets in the Former French Concession and Old Town are ideal for walking.

By Metro

See Map opposite. (8621) 28907777. www.shmetro.com. The Shanghai metro has eight separate lines. Prices are calculated according to distance (2–9 yuans). Be sure to keep your ticket until you exit the station. Metro lines generally operate from 6am–midnight.
Line 1 (5:30am–11pm) serves the Shanghai Railway Station, People's Square, the Former French Concession and Xujiahui.
Line 2 (6am–11pm) accesses Pudong, People's Square, Jing'an and Zhongshan Park (an extension is planned for Hongqiao Airport).
Line 3 (6:30am–10pm) stops at the Shanghai Railway Station, Baoxing Dong Lu and the Hongkou Stadium, but otherwise is not particularly useful for tourists.
Line 4 (5:30am–8pm) partly follows the same route as Line 3, then crosses the Huangpu River to Pudong; other than stops at the railway station and the stadium, it is of little interest for tourists.
Line 5 (6am–10:30pm) extends south of Line 1, farther away from downtown. **Line 6** (6am–9pm) accesses Shijida Dao, Minshen Lu and Wuzhou Avenue.
Line 8 (6am–10pm) stops at the Hongkou Stadium and People's Square. **Line 9** (6am–10pm) extends southwest of Lines 3 and 4. The high-speed (267mph) **Maglev Line** connects Pudong

Airport to the Longyang Road metro station in just 8min, with departures every 15min between 6:45am and 5pm (every 20min 5pm–9pm, 30min 9pm– 9:30pm); 50 yuans one-way, round-trip (same day) 80 yuans.

ACCESSIBILITY

Almost all buildings have elevators; sidewalk ramps are numerous (except for underground or elevated passageways). A limited number of public restrooms, fine hotels and museums provide handicapped access. **China Disabled Persons' Federation**: www.cdpf.org.cn.

BASIC INFORMATION
Accommodations

For suggested lodgings, see HOTELS. The Shanghai Municipal Tourism Administration maintains an online **hotel directory**, which lists websites, phone numbers and addresses for Shanghai's hotels.
Hotel Reservations – Many of the city's major hotels can be booked online on their own websites.
Hostels – A bed in a dorm-style room starts as low as 50 yuans. www.hostels.com/cn.sh.html.

Business Hours

Banks – Banks are open weekdays from 9am–5pm, and some have reduced hours on Saturday.
Shops – Department stores, larger shops, and malls are open daily 10am–10pm.
Pharmacies – Hours are generally 9am–6pm. Bring the medicines you take on a regular basis, but be aware that good medicines are normally available in China. Minor symptoms are routinely addressed with herbal medicines.

SHANGHAI METRO (2009)

Legend (line numbers):
1
2
3
4
5
6
7
8
9

Stations and labels (as shown on map):

TIELI RD, YOUYI RD, JIANGYANG RD N., BAOYANG RD, GANGCHENG RD, SHUICHAN RD, WAIGAOQIAO FREE TRADE ZONE N., FUJIN RD, SONGBIN RD, HANGJIN RD, YOUYI RD W., SONGFA RD, ZHANGHUABANG, SHIGUANG RD, WAIGAOQIAO FREE TRADE ZONE S., BAON HIGHWAY, CHANGJIANG RD S., SHOUHAI RD, GONGFU XINCUN, YINGAO RD W., NENJIANG RD, WUZHOU RD, HULAN RD, XIANGYING RD, DONGJING RD, TONGHE XINCUN, HUANGXING PARK, JUFENG RD, GONGKANG RD, JIANGWAN TOWN, MIDDLE YANJI RD, HUANGXING RD, WULIAN RD, PENGPU XINCUN, DABAISHU, JIANGPU RD, BOXING RD, WENSHUI RD, CHIFENG RD, SIPING RD, ANSHAN XINCUN, JINQIAO RD, SHANGHAI CIRCUS WORLD, HONGKOU FOOTBALL STADIUM, XIZANG RD N., ZHONGXING RD, QUYANG RD, YUNSHAN RD, YANCHANG RD, ZHONGSHAN RD N., LINPING RD, DALIAN RD, DEPING RD, ZHONGTAN RD, SHANGHAI RAILWAY STATION, DONG BAOXING RD, YANGSHUPU RD, BEIYANGJING RD, ZHENPING RD, BAOSHAN RD, HAILUN RD, QUFU RD, HUJIAZUI, PUDONG AVENUE, YUANSHEN STADIUM, CAOYANG RD, HANZHONG RD, XINZHA RD, NANJING RD E., MINSHENG RD, JINSHAJIANG RD, ZHONGSHAN PARK, JING'AN TEMPLE, NANJING RD W., PEOPLE'S SQUARE, DONGCHANG RD, CENTURY AVENUE, SHANGHAI SCI & TECH MUSEUM, SONGHONG RD, ZHONGSHAN PARK, DASHUE, BEIXINJING, WEINING RD, JIANGSU RD, CHANGSHU RD, HUANGPI RD S., LACIXIMEN, PUDIAN RD, ZHANGJIANG HI-TECH PARK, LOUSHANGUAN RD, SHANXI RD S., MADANG RD, LUJIABANG RD, PUDIAN RD, CENTURY PARK, YAN'AN RD W., HENGSHAN RD, XIZANG RD S., LANCUN, LONGYANG RD, Maglev, HONGQIAO RD, DAMUQIAO RD, NANPU BRIDGE, TANGQIAO RD, PUDONG INT'L, YISHAN RD, XUJIAHUI, SHANGHAI STADIUM, LUBAN RD, LINYI, SHANGHAI CHILDREN'S MEDICAL CENTER, CAOHEJING HI-TECH PARK, SHANGHAI INDOOR STADIUM, DONG'AN RD, (ZHOU JIA DU), XINCUN, HECHUAN RD, CAOXI RD, LONGCAO RD, YAOHUA RD, GAOKE RD W., XINGZHONG RD, CAOBAO LU, CHENGSHAN RD, DONGMING RD, ZHONGCHUN RD, QIBAO, SHANGHAI SOUTH RAILWAY STA., SHILONG RD, YANGSI, SHANGNAN RD, GAOQING RD, JIUTING, JINJIANG PARK, (JIYANG RD), HUAXIA RD W., SIJING, LIANHUA RD, LINGYAN RD S., SHESHAN, WAIHUAN RD, LINZHAO XICUN, DONGJING, XINZHUANG, CHUNSHEN RD, SONGJIANG UNIVERSITY TOWN, YINDU RD, LUHENG RD, SONGJIANG XINCHENG, ZHUANQIAO, PUJIANG TOWN, BEIQIAO, JIANGYUE RD, JIANCHUAN RD, LIANHANG RD, DONGCHUAN RD, AEROSPACE MUSEUM, WENJING RD, JINPING RD, MINHANG DEVELOPMENT ZONE, HUANING RD

Opening Spring 2010
6
7
9
Expo line (13)

Updated late 2009

Many pharmacies dispense both traditional and Western medicines. **Huaihai Pharmacy** – 528 Huaihai Zhong Lu, off Chongqing Nan Lu, in the Former French Concession. (021) 53822101. Open 24hrs/day.

Electricity

Electricity is supplied at 220 volts. American visitors will need a universal adapter for two- and three-pin round or flat plugs.

Internet

Most hotels offer Internet access. **Cybercafes** are plentiful, although they have a tendency to appear and disappear without warning. Several places to try:

Shanghai Library – 1555 Huaihai Zhong Lu, off Gaolan Lu. (021) 64455555. 9am–8:30pm (holidays 4pm). www.library.sh.cn/english. No food, beverages or smoking allowed. 4 yuans/hr.

Cyber Bar & Café – 77 Jiangning Lu, off Nanjing Xi Lu, Jing'an. (021) 62173321. Noisy; open 24hrs/day. 5 yuans/hr.

Arch – 439 Wukang Lu, near Huaihai Lu. (021) 6466 0807. Open 8am–1:30am. www.archcafe. com.cn. Popular cafe near the Former French Concession; free Wi-Fi access (bring your laptop).

Mail

Expect mail to foreign destinations to take a week to arrive. Postage rates: 4.5 yuans for postcards; 6 yuans for letters. Post offices, signage and mailboxes are dark-green, the official postal color.

Money/Currency

The principal unit of currency is the *renminbi* (literally "people's money") or the **yuan** (CNY or RMB), divided into 10 *jiaos*. The currency's value is tied to the dollar, the euro, the yen and the South Korean won. In January 2010, $1 US dollar was equivalent to 6.83 yuans. The Chinese don't normally use the word "yuan" in spoken expression, instead using the term *kuai* (meaning, literally, "monetary unit").

Currency Exchange – Chinese currency can only be exchanged within China, but it may be possible to purchase a small amount of yuans outside the country; contact your bank or a local currency exchange outlet to see if they have yuans available. Within China, you can exchange foreign currency at branch banks, airports and hotels (expect the latter to have higher fees). For up-to-date exchange rates, access **www.xe.com**. Keep your receipt to allow you to exchange any remaining yuans (up to half the original amount) when you leave the country. Have your passport with you for all currency exchange transactions.

Credit Cards – Major credit cards are accepted in large hotels, department stores, and large entertainment venues. Street markets, and the smaller hotels, shops and restaurants often do not accept credit cards.

Traveler's Checks – Traveler's checks in foreign currency can be exchanged for yuans at all exchange outlets. American Express traveler's checks offer reimbursement within 24 hours in case of theft, and have no expiration date. Sign your checks as soon as you receive them.

ATM – ATM machines and currency-exchange desks are found at Pudong airport and on the Bund: HSBC, Bank of China, Shanghai Pudong Development Bank, and others. Check to see if the name of your card is indicated on the machine. Visa, Premier, Cirrus, PLUS and Master Card are the most widely accepted. Before departing, get the telephone number of the card's issuing bank to call from China in case of card loss or theft.

Public Toilets

Always keep a little toilet paper with you, as public toilets, which are often crude, don't provide it. In general, department stores, malls and large hotels have public restrooms that reflect Western standards.

Smoking

Smoking is permitted in public places in Shanghai. Few restaurants have nonsmoking sections, but some major Western chain hotels offer smoke-free rooms.

Taxes and Tips

Shanghai has no **sales tax**. Some hotels add a 15 percent service charge to customer bills, and a few restaurants add a 10 percent service fee, but **tipping** is not expected in Shanghai, except by tour guides and tour drivers.

Telephone

In China, **cell phone** numbers begin with 13 and 15 and are 11 digits in length. The country code for China is 86; the city code for Shanghai is 021. To dial a **local number** in Shanghai, omit the 021 city code and dial only the 8 digits. www.yellowpage.com.cn/E/code/

Public telephone in Shanghai

© centrill/iStockphoto.com

index.htm lists area codes for all of China. To call Shanghai from the US, dial 011 (international access code) + 86 + 21 + 8-digit number. To call the US or Canada, dial 00 + country code 1 + 3-digit area code + 7-digit number.

Water

Drink only bottled water; do not drink tap water or have ice.

Important Numbers	
Emergency (fire, ambulance)	**119/120**
Emergency (police)	**110**
Medical Referral: Ruijin Hospital	(021) 64370045
Pharmacy (24hrs/day)	(021) 53822101
Telephone Number Inquiry	114
Weather	12121

"CITY ON THE SEA"

Shanghai sits at a latitude of 31.14 degrees north and a longitude of 121.29 degrees east on the Pacific Ocean, off the East China Sea. Lying mid-point along China's east coast, where the Yangtze River meets the sea, Shanghai literally means "city on the sea." Its strategic location amid all this water has helped make it the largest port in China.

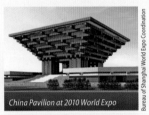

China Pavilion at 2010 World Expo

Bureau of Shanghai World Expo Coordination

Shanghai is a thoroughly modern metropolis of nearly 19 million people, but without much history, compared to Bejing. Yet, in just 150 years, Shanghai has assumed the role of the nation's commercial capital and the symbol of modern China. It holds a unique place in Chinese history because it owes its emergence to the influx of Westerners in the 19C.

The Huangpu and Suzhou rivers, which flowed to the sea, were redirected to the **Yangtze River** in the 12C, giving Shanghai control of the mouth of China's richest waterway. The late 17C saw the opening of trade with Japan and Southeast Asia. By the mid-19C, Shanghai was home to 300,000 people and ranked as the principal port in the region. The victory of the Western powers over the Qing dynasty in the **Opium Wars** culminated in the signing in 1842 of the **Treaty of Nanjing** (or Nanking), which opened Shanghai to unrestricted foreign trade and resulted in the **concessions**: land areas that, while formally part of China, were administered and populated by an occupying foreign power. The French concession was governed by its consul; the British and American concessions eventually combined into the **International Settlement**, administered by a council of landowners.

Shanghai's first fortunes were reaped from opium, real-estate

Shanghai's New Millennium Debut

From May to October 2010, Shanghai will host the **2010 World Expo**. Some 70 million attendees are expected over the six-month period. To date, 241 countries are participating. Some 42 new projects are being constructed by the city, including a new tunnel under the Huangpu River. More than 20,000 events and performances will take place in some 35 venues during the Expo. Straddling both river-banks, the two-square-mile Expo site lies south of the city center, near the Nanpu Bridge; the majority of acres are on the Pudong side. The Expo theme, "Better City, Better Life," embodies the city's concern with sustainable living in an urban setting. Michelin, a leading world tire manufacturer and publisher of travel guides, will have an exhibit on its green technology in the France pavilion.

speculation and finance, with bankers taking advantage of the vast amounts of money flowing through the city. Chinese and Western powers developed shipbuilding, **textiles** and food products industries. By 1915 Shanghai led the country in foreign trade, and 1.3 million people (15,000 of them Western expatriates) lived in the city. The **1911 Revolution** that overthrew the Chinese emperor was financed in large part by Chinese elites based in Shanghai. In 1921 the **Communist Party** was founded in the French Concession. Anti-imperialist protests culminated in Shanghai in 1927 in armed rebellion, which was suppressed by **Chiang Kai-shek**, leader of the Chinese Nationalist Party (the **Kuomintang**). Following his rise to power, organized crime flourished openly. Vice was rampant, and in the 1920s and 30s, the city of wealth became a city of sin, filled with opium dens and brothels. **World War II** brought abrupt change. In 1937 the war's fiercest battle between the Chinese and the Japanese was fought in Shanghai. The Japanese emerged victorious, and more than 100,000 Chinese lost their lives. Almost completely destroyed, the city was quickly occupied by the Japanese; Chinese residents took refuge in the Western concession, tripling its population to 4.5 million. With the Japanese defeat in World War II, all of Shanghai, including the foreign territories, reverted to Chinese control. In 1949 the city came under Communist control. Party leader **Mao Zedong** took a dim view of the capitalist

city. It played a significant role, however, in Mao's 1966 **Cultural Revolution** when three leaders of Shanghai's Communist faction allied themselves with Mao's wife Jiang Qing, becoming known as the "Gang of Four."

After Mao's death in 1976, the reformist **Deng Xiaoping** came to power, but Shanghai did not see true economic recovery until it was authorized to create the **Pudong** in 1990. This new economic zone, which implemented growth-inducing measures, such as tax breaks and suspension of tariffs and duties, has seen remarkable foreign investment and has driven Shanghai to its present-day position as the engine of the Chinese economy. The city now accounts for 11 percent of China's **gross domestic product**. In addition to a massive working population, students and visitors flock here, engendering even more growth (along with a speculative real-estate bubble and the striking transformation of the urban landscape). Ever in pursuit of the next big thing, Shanghai is hosting the **World Exposition of 2010** (see box opposite page).

"CITY ON THE SEA"

DISTRICTS

Although Shanghai is an immense city, much of its architectural and cultural diversity is confined to the urban core, which centers on both banks of the Huangpu River. For sightseeing purposes, the following six geographical areas capture the major attractions of interest to visitors: The Bund, People's Square (including Nanjing Street), the Former French Concession, Old Town, the Pudong and Xujiahui, each with its own character and rhythm. Most streets are signed in English as well as Chinese, so wear comfortable shoes and see these districts on foot. It's often the nooks and crannies that hold rewarding discoveries.

THE BUND★★★

Derived from a Hindu word for "embankment," the Bund runs along the left bank of the Huangpu River, from the Waibaidu Bridge in the north to the edge of Yu Garden in the south. The Bund is also the name of the lengthy **boulevard** (Zhongshan Dong Lu) that stretches north to south along the river's Huangpu Park. The historic waterfront, beautifully illuminated at night, is lined with grand **colonial buildings** born of Western-style capitalism in the 1920s and 30s. This iconic strip of real estate has been featured in many movies in which Shanghai has provided the setting.

Facing the new skyscrapers of the Pudong, the Bund has once again attracted prestigious banking firms and international companies that embody Shanghai's new-found prosperity. A pedestrian walkway called the **promenade★★★** daily draws a colorful parade of residents, tourists, hawkers, buskers, kite flyers, tai chi practitioners with red fans in hand, and even ballroom dancers.

Just west of the Bund, the aging façades from the time of the International Concessions hold within all manner of small markets, diverse restaurants and fashionable hang-outs. Pedestrians and cyclists crowd the streets.

The Bund at night

The Best of the Bund

Here's a preview of splendid buildings you'll see along the Bund, many dating to the 1920s and 30s.

Peace Hotel (left) and the Bank of China (right)

David Shen Kai/Apa Publications

Bank of China★★

A majestic adaptation of the sky-scraper, with Chinese motifs, this 1937 building (No. 23) sports a low pyramidal roof and traditionally patterned windows. The building appears somewhat truncated, since it was originally planned to reach 34 floors, but Victor Sassoon (see below) used his influence to keep the new building at a scale that would not diminish the grandeur of his nearby Sassoon House (now the Peace Hotel). Consequently, the Bank of China numbers only 17 floors and is shorter than its eminent neighbor.

Peace Hotel★★

See HOTELS. Under renovation until 2010 when it is slated to open as The Fairmont Peace Hotel. This Art Deco building (No. 20) embodies Shanghai's past opulence and the power of its owner, 20C British entrepreneur **Victor Sassoon**. Topped by a green copper pyramidal roof, the former Sassoon House (1929) once sheltered the private apartments of his family and incorporated the famous **Cathay Hotel** in its upper floors. A ballroom, restaurant, bar and reading room hosted dignitaries and celebrities during the hotel's pre-1949 heyday.

Shanghai Pudong Development Bank★★

Recognizable by its broad façade topped by a central dome, this massive building (No. 12) was erected in 1923 by the Hong Kong and Shanghai Banking Corp. (HSBC). When the Communists took over Shanghai in 1949, it was transformed into the headquarters of the municipality. In the 1990s, the Shanghai Pudong Development Bank purchased it, and the building again served as a bank. Its interior includes Art Deco lamps, chandeliers, and counters of Italian black marble. Still visible in the hall are the original frescoes representing allegories of the international cities.

Touring Tip

The mile-long walk along the Bund is a must-do, both during the day as well as at night. Go there early in the morning (around 6am or 7am) on a weekday to see the Shanghainese, often with a fan in each hand, do tai chi exercises. Return there in the evening to admire the city lights that make both banks of the Huangpu River glow.

DISTRICTS

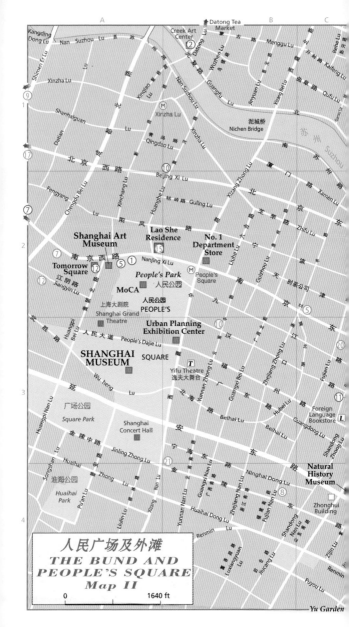

THE BUND AND PEOPLE'S SQUARE

人民广场及外滩
THE BUND AND
PEOPLE'S SQUARE
Map II

0   1640 ft

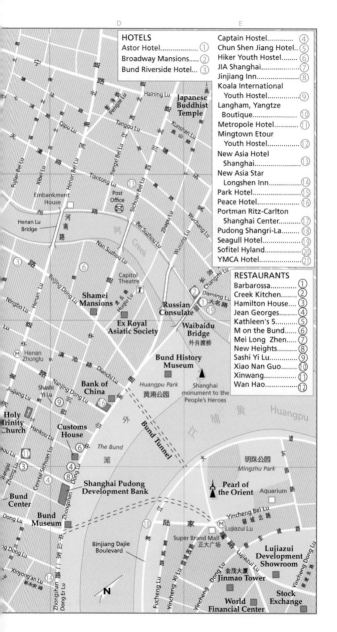

HOTELS

Astor Hotel.................. ①
Broadway Mansions..... ②
Bund Riverside Hotel... ③
Captain Hostel............. ④
Chun Shen Jiang Hotel.. ⑤
Hiker Youth Hostel........ ⑥
JIA Shanghai................ ⑦
Jinjiang Inn................. ⑧
Koala International
  Youth Hostel............. ⑨
Langham, Yangtze
  Boutique................. ⑩
Metropole Hotel........... ⑪
Mingtown Etour
  Youth Hostel............. ⑫
New Asia Hotel
  Shanghai................. ⑬
New Asia Star
  Longshen Inn............ ⑭
Park Hotel................... ⑮
Peace Hotel................. ⑯
Portman Ritz-Carlton
  Shanghai Center........ ⑰
Pudong Shangri-La...... ⑱
Seagull Hotel............... ⑲
Sofitel Hyland............. ⑳
YMCA Hotel................. ㉑

RESTAURANTS

Barossa................. ①
Creek Kitchen............ ②
Hamilton House.... ③
Jean Georges.......... ④
Kathleen's 5............ ⑤
M on the Bund....... ⑥
Mei Long Zhen...... ⑦
New Heights........... ⑧
Sashi Yi Lu.............. ⑨
Xiao Nan Guo........ ⑩
Xinwang................. ⑪
Wan Hao................ ⑫

Haining Lu
Japanese Buddhist Temple
Qipu Lu
Tanggu Lu
Kunshan Lu
Penglai Lu
Beijing Bei Lu
Fujian Bei Lu
Kibei Lu
Tanggu Lu
Henan Bei Lu
Trantong Lu
Tiantong Lu
Sichuan Bei Lu
Embankment House
Post Office
Henan Lu Bridge
河南 路
Nan Suzhou Lu
Suzhou Creek
Bei Suzhou Lu
Zhapu Lu
Wuchang Lu
河
Beijing Dong Lu
Capitol Theatre
Changzhi Lu
Daming Lu
Shamei Mansions
Russian Consulate
Ningbo Lu
Henan Lu
Jiangxi Lu
Ex Royal Asiatic Society
Waibaidu Bridge
外白渡桥
Henan Zhonglu
Dianchi Lu
Bund History Museum
Nanjing Dong Lu
Bank of China
Huangpu Park
黄浦公园
Shanghai monument to the People's Heroes
Jiujiang Lu
Shashi Yi Lu
Holy Trinity Church
Hankou Lu
Customs House
The Bund
外
Huangpu 黄浦
Bund Tunnel
滩
Central Sichuan Lu
Shanghai Pudong Development Bank
Pearl of the Orient
Aquarium
明珠公园
Mingzhu Park
Bund Center
Bund Museum
Dong Lu
Zhongshan
Yincheng Bei Lu
Lujiazui Lu
陆 家
Super Brand Mall
正大广场
Lujiazui Road
Lujiazui Development Showroom
Binjiang Dajie Boulevard
Fucheng Lu
Yincheng Xi Lu
Yincheng
Dong Lu
金茂大厦 Jinmao Tower
World Financial Center
Stock Exchange
Zhongshan Dong Yi Lu
Xinyong'an Lu
新永安 路
N

37

Best Views of the Bund

From the ground, the best viewpoint of the Bund is in **Huangpu Park** from the **People's Heroes of Shanghai Memorial,** which commemorates the liberation of the city on May 25, 1949, when the Communists took over. The park is a popular place for flying kites.

For an elevated view of the district, head to **New Heights** on the top floor of the Three on the Bund complex *(see RESTAURANTS, No. 3 The Bund, 7th floor; 021-63210909; www.threeonthebund.com).* The restaurant's outdoor terrace is famed for its vantage point overlooking the historic Bund, the Pudong and the Huangpu River. Have lunch or an evening cocktail there while you enjoy the 180-degree views, made even more fabulous by the neon lights of the city after dark.

Two blocks south, the former **Union Building** (1916), capped by a columned corner turret, houses **Three on the Bund** *(open daily 11am–11pm; 021 63215757; www.threeonthebund.com),* which includes upscale restaurants, luxury shops and the Evian Spa *(see SPAS).*

Customs House★

This eight-story building is the only structure on the Bund that has retained its original purpose. It still houses the Customs Service, charged with collecting taxes. The structure has been rebuilt twice,

Shanghai Pudong Development Bank (left) and the Customs House (right)

from a wooden structure in 1864 to a British neo-Gothic palace (1891) to the current Neoclassical edifice (1927) with its tiered clock tower.

Behind the Bund

Just west of the Bund, the narrower streets hold a few architectural marvels inventoried by the municipality but often neglected by their owners. The building of the former **Royal Asiatic Society** (1932) is a mixture of Art Deco and traditional Chinese patterns. Slightly ahead, the façade of the **Shamei Mansions** (1918) is covered by stucco and ironwork. At the intersection of Jiangxi Lu and Fuzhou Lu stand interesting façades around a square. The **Metropole Hotel** (1934) and the former **Hamilton Hotel** (1934) each present a concave façade *(see HOTELS).* On the opposite side, the former **Commercial Bank of China** (1934) housed the administration of the International Concession. Beside it stands the home of the **Shanghai Municipal Council**. At 201 Jiujiang Lu, the **Holy Trinity Church** *(under renovation)* was built in 1869 by

David Shen Kai/Apa Publications

English architect Sir George Gilbert Scott in the Gothic Revival style. Visible from the Bund, the **Bund Center** (2002) rises 44 floors, capped by a roof resembling a giant lotus flower, the symbol of prosperity in China.

Over the Bridge

At the northern end of the Bund, the **Waibaidu Bridge** (1906), which spans the Suzhou Creek, is a grim reminder of the Japanese invasion of Shanghai. It served as a border between the International Concession and the Japanese quarter of Hongkou. Fleeing from the invaders, thousands of Chinese crossed the bridge to seek shelter in the International Concession. The old steel bridge was recently reconstructed for today's heavy traffic and reopened in 2009; it's quieter now, animated only by a few street vendors who sell eggs and tofu. At the end of the bridge, the **Russian Consulate** (1917) flies the colors of Russia. Flanking the bridge are two hotels of note:

Astor House★

Shanghai's oldest hotel has been rebuilt several times and moved

People's Heroes of Shanghai Memorial

©Robert Van Beets/www.istockphoto.com

once since 1846. Today the 1910 version has corridors with parquet floors, photographs of famous guests and the ballroom that hosted the first transactions of the Shanghai Stock Exchange (1990) *(see HOTELS)*.

Broadway Mansions

Victor Sassoon had this Art Deco residence (1934) built in line with the Bund on the opposite side of Suzhou Creek. In 1951 it was converted into a hotel *(see HOTELS)*.

Museums in the Mix

The Bund is the site of three of the city's many museums. At the north end, at the base of the People's Heroes monument in Huangpu Park, you'll find the **Bund History Museum**, which exhibits photographs and artifacts relating to the area *(may be closed for renovation)*. At the other end, to the south, the **Bund Museum** occupies the base of the 1907 Signal Tower that first guided river traffic and was later moved and rebuilt to provide weather information. It has some historic photographs of the old waterfront, and on a clear day you can get a good view from the tower. Inland about three blocks, at the corner of Yan'an Dong Lu and Henan Zhong Lu, sits the **Natural History Museum**, which has a collection, among other items, of dinosaur skeletons. *For details about all three museums, see MUSEUMS.*

DISTRICTS

PEOPLE'S SQUARE AND NANJING LU ★★★

The most honored institutions of the city occupy the real estate of People's Square, once the British horse-racing grounds and now the symbolic and geographic center of Shanghai. Recognizable in the middle of this combination plaza and park is massive city hall. Spreading north from city hall lies the green space known as People's Park. All around it, buildings such as Tomorrow Square and the Park Hotel compete to be the tallest. South of the park sit the eye-catching modern structure that is the Grand Theatre *(see NIGHTLIFE)* and the immense Shanghai Museum with its distinctive roof and stunning collection of Chinese art. Crossing the square in an east-west direction, lengthy Nanjing Lu is a major shopping mecca, known for its malls and stores.

Nanjing Road

Top Three Things to Do in People's Square

Visit a Museum

The district is a hub for several of the city's major museums, which attract thousands of visitors. The vast Shanghai Museum may be especially crowded when you go.

Shanghai Museum ★★★

See MUSEUMS. World famous for its bronzes, ceramics and paintings, this museum possesses some 120,000 works covering 4,000 years of history. The building (1994) was inspired by Chinese cosmogony: a square base symbolizing the earth topped by a round roof representing the sky.

MoCA Shanghai

Open Sat–Thu 10am–6pm (Wed til 10pm). 20 yuans. (021) 63279900. www.mocashanghai.org.

Opened in 2006, the Museum of Contemporary Art Shanghai (MoCA) is the city's first private museum. It hosts temporary exhibits of contemporary art, mostly by international artists. Recalling the greenhouse it once was, the redesigned glass-box building lets in abundant light for art viewing, and complements the surrounding grounds of People's Park.

Shanghai Art Museum

See MUSEUMS. This museum is housed in the former clubhouse

Inside MoCA Shanghai

(1933) of the racetrack that stood where People's Square does now. Its clock tower rang out the start of each race. The museum mounts the largest temporary exhibits in Shanghai as well as rotating displays of contemporary works. Every two years, it hosts the prestigious **Biennale** *(see CALENDAR OF EVENTS)*. Take a break in the museum store or in the fifth-floor restaurant, **Kathleen's 5** *(see RESTAURANTS)*.

Urban Planning Exhibition Center

Open daily 9am–5pm (Sat–Sun til 6pm). 30 yuans. (021) 63722077. www.supec.org.

This handsome five-story structure of glass and steel (2000) refracts the light differently depending on the hour of the day. On the front of the building a counter records the days remaining until World Expo 2010 *(see INTRODUCTION)*. Museum exhibits tell the history of Shanghai's urban development, but the most interesting display is a gigantic scale model of the city of Shanghai in 2020, as envisioned by urban planners.

Stroll in the Park

The **People's Park** *(see PARKS AND GARDENS)* makes a lovely setting for a leisurely stroll. This green space features a lake, flower beds, a rock garden, benches and paved pathways for the enjoyment of the community, especially local

Best Viewpoint

Don't miss the view of the People's Square from the terrace on the eighth floor of the **Grand Theatre** *(see NIGHTLIFE)*. Come here in the afternoon, rather than in the morning, when the sun is in the west. This star of Shanghai's new modernity was designed by French architect Jean-Marie Charpentier, and built in the shape of the king's Chinese character. Sharing with the Urban Planning Center the same distinctive conceptual (strict respect for the rules of geomancy and *feng shui*) and architectural (steel, glass and light) features, the theater stands as one of the jewels of the People's Square.

residents, who come here to fly kites and feed the pigeons. The park is actually divided into two sections: the southern part serves as the grounds for the massive Shanghai Museum *(see MUSEUMS)*, complete with ornamental gardens; frequented by sports enthusiasts and lovers, among other habitués, the northern area is home to MoCA Shanghai and city hall.

North of the park, Nanjing Lu draws a curve that follows what was the former racecourse: in the middle of the curve, the 23-story **Park Hotel★★** (1933) *(see HOTELS)* is still one of the most elegant buildings in Shanghai, even though its former grandeur has been diminished. Until the 1980s, its glazed-brick pyramidal profile dominated the city. A taller skyscraper overlooks the park: the **Tomorrow Square** tower is 60 stories high and features an upper section that rotates 90 degrees.

Go Shopping

Nanjing Lu, whose midpoint is the People's Park, used to be called China's "Number One Shopping Street." In recent years other streets have become stronger competitors in terms of offering nicer stores *(see SHOPPING)*, but the thoroughfare should not be missed, if only for the local color it provides.

Nanjing Dong Lu

East from the People's Square, the pedestrian part of Nanjing Lu is dotted with the first department stores of Shanghai—and China—which were established here in the 1910s. Competing for customers were the "Big Four" merchantile houses. Among them, the **No. 1 Department Store** (1936) is the most emblematic, with a curved and glazed façade *(northeast corner of the square)*. It was the first department store in China to be equipped with escalators.

People's Square with the Park Hotel in background on right

On the other side of the pedestrian area, the former **Continental Emporium** (No. 345) housed the **Chinese Native Goods Company** on its first two floors. One of the first Chinese department stores, the firm sold only Chinese goods.

Nanjing Xi Lu

This area west of the square is much more modern in appearance and boasts the biggest shopping malls in the city. Proud of its 66-story tower, **Plaza 66** (2001) has attracted the luxury haute couture brands such as Bulgari, Chanel, Dior, Gaultier and Vuitton. It's probably the quietest and the most comfortable mall downtown.

One block west, the Soviet-style **Exhibition Palace** faces the Westernized **Shanghai Centre**. The former structure was built in 1955 to celebrate the Soviet Entente (which was broken just five years later). The building incorporates symbols of the Soviet Union: corn and red stars are everywhere. In front of it, the Shanghai Centre, inaugurated in 1990, marked the beginning of a new era for Shanghai: this residential-commercial complex boasted the first ATM in town. Farther west rises the last version (2004) of the **Jing'an Buddhist Temple** (see PLACES OF WORSHIP). Founded during the third century, it is perfectly integrated into the area with its shops that compete with those of the nearby City Plaza. The adjacent **Paramount**, the most famous Shanghai dance hall of the 1930s, was later transformed into a theater. Today it is once again attracting dance fans who come to relive

David Shen Kai/Apa Publications

No. 1 Department Store

the ballroom's glamor days. Two indoor swimming pools, with gold furniture on their decks, are adorned with iridescent colored walls and frescoes illustrating the Roaring Twenties.

Near the intersection of Nanjing Xi Lu and Wulumuqi Bei Lu sits the **Children's Palace★★** within the former mansion (1924) of the Kadoorie family. The residence was decorated luxuriously in its heyday: its immense and famous ballroom, **Marble Hall★★**, drew its name from two gigantic chimneys created from Italian marble. After the influential Jewish family left for Hong Kong, the mansion was abandoned for many years. It was eventually chosen by Song Qingling (Sun Yat-sen's wife) as a place dedicated to sporting and creative activities for the deserving children of the city. *English tours available Wed–Sun 8:30am–5:30pm; 20 yuans; (021) 62481850.*

FORMER FRENCH CONCESSION★★

Small houses along streets rimmed with French plane trees and narrow, peaceful alleys called *lilongs* lend a human scale to the Former French Concession. A treasure trove of architectural styles, the district remains the jewel of Shanghai's residential quarters. Fashionistas go there to shop for the latest trends, expatriates sip a drink in Xintiandi before going to dine in one of the villas of the quarter, and party lovers spend the last hours of the night hanging out in one of its nightclubs.

Tree-lined Hengshan Lu

Hotels to Haunt

Two well-regarded hotels occupy grand old buildings with a history of catering to the rich and famous.

Jin Jiang Hotel★★

59 Maoming Lu. (021) 32189888. www.jinjianghotels.com.

This striking construction was financed by Victor Sassoon. The hotel *(see HOTELS)* is housed in two prestigious former residences: what was once the Cathay Mansion Hotel (1929) with a typical Victorian façade, and **Grosvenor House★★** (1935), secluded at the back of the property. This 18-story Art Deco building hosted the most important international policymakers and heads of State of the day. Along Maoming Lu, the shops were designed in the same vein as the hotel and so was the Guotai Cinema (1932; former Cathay Theatre), at the crossroads with Huaihai Zhong Lu.

Ruijin Hotel★

118 Ruijin Er Lu. (021) 64725222. www. ruijinhotelsh.com. Villa Taiyuan: 160 Taiyuan Lu.

A luxurious former family estate has been transformed into the Ruijin Hotel *(see HOTELS)* of today. The large compound once hosted guests of State visiting Shanghai in the 1950s and 60s; they were put up in the main mansion, now called the Taiyuan Villa. Three other villas sit in a park with 100-year-old cedar, pine and palm trees. The **Taiyuan Villa★★**—also known as the "villa of the happy widow"—is the most interesting building of the complex.

Located on a peaceful street and hidden behind trees, this mansard-roofed manor could be sitting in the French countryside. It was owned by Comte Maurice Frédéric Armand du Pac de Marsolies, who died a few weeks after racing in the Croisière Jaune, the first car rally between Beirut and Beijing organized by André Citroën. It is said that he was murdered by a top drug lord. Left with the villa and a large amount of money, his widow, Ginette, was known as the Merry Widow.

Sun Yat-sen's former residence

David Shen Kai/Apa Publications

Homes with History

Former Residence of Sun Yat-sen★★

7 Xiangshan. Guided tour in English daily 9am–4:30pm. 20 yuans. (021) 64372954.

Sun Yat-sen (1866–1925) was the first president of the Republic. At No. 29 on the former Molière Street, in a posh neighborhood, stands what was once the residence of Sun Yat-sen and his wife, Song Qingling, from 1918 to 1937. The typical 1920s architecture has been preserved without any modification, and the interior is still appointed with exquisite furniture and paintings. Between these walls, Sun Yat-sen wrote a large page in China's history. You will see a photograph of his wedding in Tokyo (1915) and maps annotated by the hand of Sun himself.

Not far from here is the **Former Residence of Zhou Enlai★**, Mao Zedong's second in command and prime minister of China from 1896–1976. The house was the Chinese Communist Party's general headquarters from 1946–47. The furniture belongs to

Dr. Sun Yat-sen

Sun Yat-sen (1866–1925) descended from a family of modest means in Canton. After obtaining a diploma in medicine in Hong Kong, he worked for the unity and integrity of China. He took part in uprisings in the south of the country against an imperial regime weakened by influence from the West. In 1912 he became president of the Republic of China, the first president in the history of the country. He participated in the student movement of 1919, founded the Kuomintang in 1920 and integrated the Communists in 1924 in the fight against foreign powers. The Chinese people hold him in high regard. City officials affixed to his statue at the entrance of his residence this tribute: "The man who changed China, Dr. Sun Yat-sen."

DISTRICTS

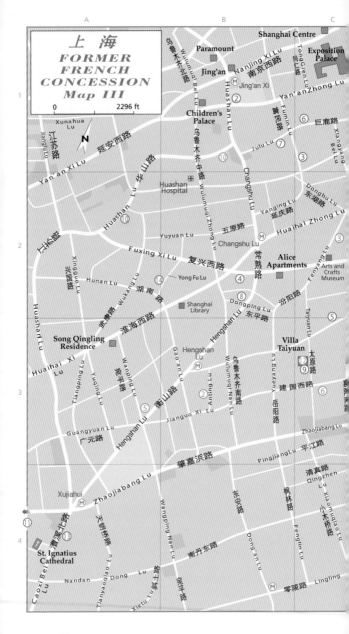

上 海
FORMER
FRENCH
CONCESSION
Map III

0   2296 ft

Shanghai Centre

Paramount

Jing'an

Exposition Palace

Nanjing Xi Lu 南京西路

Jing'an Xi

Yan'an Zhong Lu

Wulumuqi Bei Lu 乌鲁木齐北路

Huashan Lu

Fumin Lu 富民路

巨鹿路

Xiangyang Bei Lu

Children's Palace

Xunhua Lu

江苏路

Jiangsu Lu

延安西路

Yan'an Xi Lu

华山路

Huashan Lu

乌鲁木齐中路

Wulumuqi Zhong Lu

Changshu Lu

五原路

Yuyuan Lu

Huashan Hospital

延庆路

Yanqing Lu

东湖路

Donghu Lu

Huaihai Zhong Lu 淮海中路

上海图

Shangping Lu

Fuxing Xi Lu 复兴西路

常熟路

Changshu Lu

Changshu Lu

Alice Apartments

Arts and Crafts Museum

Fenyang Lu

兴国路

Xingguo Lu

Hunan Lu

Wukang Lu

Yong Fu Lu

Shanghai Library

Dongping Lu 东平路

汾阳路

Fenyang Lu

Taiyuan Lu

华山路

Huashan Lu

武康路

Wukang Lu

湖南路

Hunan Lu

淮海西路

Song Qingling Residence

Hengshan Lu

Hengshan Lu 衡山路

乌鲁木齐南路

Wulumuqi Nan Lu

Villa Taiyuan

太原路

建国西路

Jianguo Xi Lu

Yueyang Lu

岳阳路

Yuqing Lu

Tianping Lu

Wenping Lu

Gao'an Lu

Anting Lu

Jianguo Xi Lu 建国西路

Zhaojiabang Lu

Guangyuan Lu 广元路

Hengshan Lu

衡山路

Jianguo Xi Lu

Huaihai Xi Lu

Tianping Lu

肇嘉浜路

Zhaojiabang Lu

PingjiangLu 平江路

Xujiahui

Zhaojiabang Lu 肇嘉浜路

清真寺

Qingzhen Lu

枫林路

Fenglin Lu

小木桥路

Xiaomuqiao Lu

St. Ignatius Cathedral

Caoxi Bei Lu

漕溪北路

天钥桥路

Tianyaoqiao Lu

Nandan

Tianyaoqiao Dong Lu

漕溪路

南丹东路

Nandan Dong Lu

斜土路

Xietu Lu

肇嘉浜路

Wangping Nan Lu

东安路

Dong'an Lu

Lingling Lu

零陵路

SHANGHAI MUSEUM

ⓂPeople's Square

毛泽东故居
Mao Zedong Residence

Weihai Lu 威海路

黄陂北路 Huangpi Bei Lu

Wusheng Lu 武胜路

Xizang Nan Lu 西藏南路

延安东路 Yan'an Dong Lu

中路 茂名北路 Maoming Bei Lu

石门一路 Shimen Yi Lu

巨鹿路 Julu Lu

Site of Second CCP Meeting

金陵西路 Jin ling Xi Lu

金陵中路 Jinling Zhong Lu

柳林路 Liulin Lu

西藏南路 Xizang Nan Lu

Lyceum Theatre

Verdun Terrace

Changle Lu 长乐路

黄陂南路 Huangpi Nan Lu

Huangpi Nan Lu 黄陂 南路

⑨ ④ **Jin Jiang Hotel**

茂名南路 Maoming Nan Lu

淮海中路 Huaihai Zhong Lu

Former French Sports Club

Ⓜ Shaanxi Nan Lu ⑧

南昌路 Nanchang Lu

College français

太仓路 Taicang Lu

⑦

Xintiandi
兴业路

Site of CCP Inaugural Meeting

Xingya Lu

Zihong Lu 自忠路

Dongtai Lu 东台路

①

陕西南路 Maoming Nan Lu

Gaolan Lu 香山路

Xiangshan Lu 香山路

Fuxing Park
复兴公园

Chongqing Nan Lu 重庆南路

Fuxing Zhong Lu 复兴中路

Danshui Lu 淡水路

Shunchang Lu 顺昌路

制造局路 Zhizaoju Lu

Cité Bourgogne

陕西南路

Sun Yat-sen Residence

思南路 Sinan Lu

Zhou Enlai Residence

重庆南路 Chongqing Nan Lu

淡水路 Danshui Lu

Ⓗ **Ruijin Hotel**

瑞金二路 Ruijin Er Lu

Yongjia Lu 永嘉路

Flower Market

Jianguo Zhong Lu 建国中路

Jianguo Dong Lu 建国东路

建国东路 Jianguo Dong Lu

Zhizaoju Lu 制造局路

Shaanxi Nan Xi

Ⓜ

瑞金二路 Ruijin Er Lu

Taikang Lu 泰康路

Xujiahui Lu 徐家汇路

蒙自路 Mengzi Lu

局门路 Jumen Lu

uo Shaanxi Nan Xi

Liyuan Lu 丽园路

Luban Lu 鲁班路

Mengzi Lu 蒙自路

Ruijin Nan Lu

鲁班路 Luban Lu

斜土路 XietuLu

RESTAURANTS

1931	①
Bali Laguna	②
Bao Luo	③
Cang Lang Ting.	④
Dian Shi Zhai	⑤
Mesa-Manifesto.	⑥
People 7 and Shintori	⑦
Sasha's	⑧
Taiyuan Villa Restaurant	⑨
Xian Yue Hien	⑩
Xinjiang Fengwei	⑪
Ye Shanghai	⑫
Ye Olde Station	⑬
Yongfoo Elite	⑭

Chajing Lu

Zhongshan Nan Lu

HOTELS

88 Xintiandi	①
Anting Villa	②
Education Hotel	③
Grosvenor House	④
Hengshan Picardie Hotel	⑤
Hotel N°9	⑥
Lapis Casa	⑦
New Westlake Club	⑧
Okura Garden Hotel	⑨
Old House Inn	⑩
Ruijin Hotel	⑪
Taiyuan Villa Guesthouse	⑰

that period (but is not the original) and attests to the revolutionaries' penurious living conditions.

Shaanxi Lu★

Residence of Mao Zedong: 120 Maoming Bei Lu. Open Tue–Sun 8:30am–4pm. 2 yuans. (021) 62723656.

Sitting on the outskirts of the French Concession, the **Residence of Mao Zedong** features a museum and recreations of some of the original rooms. The residence was part of a *shikumen* constructed of wood and brick *(see box opposite page)* in the commonplace *lilong*. Mao, who dwelt in seven different residences in Shanghai during the 1920s, lived in this one in 1924 with his wife and two children. At Nos. 39–45 Shaanxi Nan Lu, the **Verdun Terrace** *lilong* (1929) looks quite comfortable with its terraced houses and their small, private gardens. At No. 187 the tall, arched entry to the **Cité Bourgogne** (1930) was inspired by Chinese architecture. Behind it lies a compound of alleyways with *shikumen* housing many families. Walk farther to No. 1363 Fuxing Zhong Lu, where the **Alice Apartments★** *lilong* (1906) comprise pleasant redbrick buildings.

Other Highlights

Former French Sports Club★

Entrance at 58 Maoming Nan Lu.

Now incorporated into the high-rise **Okura Garden Hotel** *(see HOTELS)*, the magnificent home of the erstwhile French Sports Club (1926) functioned at the time as the very heart of Shanghai's French social and intellectual community. The main **staircase★** *(off the east lobby)* is by far the jewel of the place, and the Art Deco **ballroom★** should definitely be visited. The spring-mounted dance floor was once the hottest of Shanghai's night spots.

Fuxing Park★

2 Gaolan Lu. Open daily 5am–9pm in summer (6am–6pm in winter).

Established by the French in 1909, this popular park *(see PARKS AND GARDENS)*, especially beloved by families, sits apart from the main roads. Card players and mah-jong fans gather under the 100-year-old plane trees, their activities a source of amusement for passers-by. To the north the park is bordered by the former **Collège Français★** (1926), whose buildings were inspired by the architecture of Normandy, France; sumptuous woodwork covers the interior walls and ceilings of several campus buildings.

Xintiandi★

(021) 63112288. www.xintiandi.com.

The latest Chinese "revolution"—and a capitalistic one at that—has transformed some of the original alleys lying just east of Fuxing Park into Xintiandi [pronounced Shin-tee-en-dee] or "new world," with more of a 21C vibe. Many of the remaining *shikumen* today house fancy brand-name boutiques, restaurants and bars, making Xintiandi a popular shopping/entertainment mecca.

What are Shikumen?

Shikumen are two- or three-story brick town houses, each with a small courtyard or garden enclosed by a high brick wall. The word translates as "stone-hooped," a reference to the curved or swirling stone work above the door frames of these attached dwellings, or row houses. The high-density housing settlements were called *lilongs*, or literally, "neighborhoods with lanes," since the units had lanes or alleyways at the front and back. Such housing was nearly universal in Shanghai from the 1860s to the late 1940s.

In Xintiandi, be sure to visit the **Shikumen Open House Museum** *(entrance Xingya Lu; open daily 11:00am–11pm; 021 33070337; www.xintiandi. com/english/aboutus_ history3.asp)* to see seven rooms of a typical two-story *shikumen* furnished to the 1920s period.

The lanes have been spared, so far, from the hand of real estate developers, thanks to the fact that one of the buildings housed the inaugural meeting of the Chinese Communist Party in 1921. During the 1920s and 30s, Shanghai became the capital of the Communist workers. Assembled in the **house of Li Hanjun**, the 13 founding members had to flee from the police of the concession, and later finished their meeting in a small boat on a lake in the nearby Zhejiang province. Considered a major historic site, the house is closely guarded, and proper decorum on the part of visitors is expected.

Site of the Chinese Communist Party Inaugural Meeting

374 Huangpi Nan Lu. Open daily 9am–5pm. 3 yuans. (021) 53832171.

The founding members of the CCP gathered here on July 1, 1921. One of the wax figures represents Mao, standing tall as leader. Also notice the bronze canon of the Chinese imperial army, which was used during the First Opium War (1842).

Site of the Second Chinese Communist Party Meeting

30 Chengdu Lu, 7 Nong. Open daily 9am–11:30am & 1:30am–4:30pm. 3 yuans.

History buffs will want to visit this house, which stands in the shadow of the east-west elevated highway. The meeting was held in July 1922 in this *shikumen*. The proceedings laid down the fundamentals of Chinese Communism.

Courtesy of Shanghai Xintiandi

Shikumen houses in Xintiandi

OLD TOWN★★

Southwest of the Bund and bordered by the Huangpu River are the remains of the old Shanghai. Home to the local Chinese for centuries, Old Town used to be enclosed within a city wall *(see below)*.

Today it is being hastily restructured: many of the long-standing houses have been demolished for newer developments. Around the Yu Garden, which dates to the Ming dynasty, a new bazaar is sheltered beneath hundreds of curved roofs. In the same neighborhood, the Confucius Temple is surrounded by old winding alleys far from the bustle of the rest of the city. United by religious and business fervor, Old Town perpetuates a carnival-like atmosphere, with vendors selling all manner of merchandise at any time, and various temples, now reopened to the public, attract devotees and curiosity-seekers.

Old Town Highlights

Yu Garden★★

See PARKS AND GARDENS.

Yu Garden is not only a surprising haven of peace and tranquillity in the heart of one of the most populous sections of the city, it's also one of the most attractive classical gardens in all of China. It is the only remarkable historic landmark left in Shanghai.

Laid out in 1578 by the former governor of Sichuan Province for his father, the garden has survived the recent and past tumultuous transformations of the vicinity.

Booked on Sundays

The courtyard of the Confucius Temple on Wenmiao road has been the scene of a popular book fair on Sundays *(8:30am– 4:30pm)*. Here you'll find a lot of second-hand books in Chinese for sale. But if you search a bit, you may discover a tome or two in English, and of good vintage in terms of age. If the search makes you hungry, enjoy some street food from the vendors outside the temple or tea at the Huxinting Teahouse.

Bridge of Nine Turns leading to Huxinting Teahouse, Yu Garden

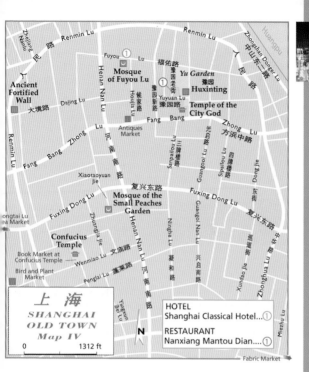

Fabric Market

Behind the garden, in a pavilion on stilts in the middle of a man-made lake, is the oldest (1855) and the most famous teahouse in China: **Huxinting Teahouse★**. It used to attract merchants and brokers who conducted business over a cup of tea. Cross the **Bridge of Nine Turns**, which zigzags supposedly to keep away evil spirits, to enjoy a calming cup of tea.

South of the teahouse stands the Taoist **Temple of the City God** (see PLACES OF WORSHIP).

Ancient Fortified Wall★

Renmin Lu at Dajing Lu.

A 150-foot section of the **old wall** is the only known remnant of the ramparts built by the Ming dynasty, and destroyed in 1912. The wall used to encircle the city to protect it from Japanese pirates. Rebuilt in 1995, a stone tower houses an **exhibit** *(open daily 9am–4:30pm; 5 yuans; 021 63852443)*, unfortunately rather run-down, that retraces *(in Chinese)* the history of the district, as well as a painting and calligraphy workshop.

DISTRICTS

51

Mosques of Old Town
See PLACES OF WORSHIP.
A discrete minaret signals the **Mosque of Fuyou Lu** (1870), which occupies a tiny courtyard: the two first rooms are packed with tables and chairs in a typical Chinese style. The prayer room lies in the back. Chinese and Arabic calligraphies hang on the walls. Covered with writings, the **Mosque of the Small Peaches Garden★** is hidden behind a green (the color of Islam) façade.

Museum of Popular Collections★
See MUSEUMS.
Located on the outskirts of Old Town, this museum is housed in the former headquarters of the **Guild of the Three Mounts★** (1909), which drew merchants from the Fujian Province (Southeast China). The building's interior has several remarkable features, and the collections comprise wide-ranging items of daily life from times past.

Ancient fortified wall on Dajing Lu
David Shen Kai/Apa Publications

Confucius Temple★
See PLACES OF WORSHIP.
This temple is located in a pretty neighborhood filled with traditional houses and crossed by narrow alleys lively with hawkers and the sounds of daily life. Inhabitants often chitchat with one another, sitting on chairs in front of their dwellings.

Confucius Temple

MUST SEE THE PUDONG

THE PUDONG★★

Facing the Bund, Shanghai's "Far East" embodies the visions of an ambitious city. The Pudong's goal was "to become an international finance center and the symbolic capital of the Far East." This urbanscape on the east side of the Huangpu River combines a free port, an international airport and soaring skyscrapers; the most compelling is the space-age Pearl of the Orient TV Tower. The new World Financial Center ranks as one of the tallest towers in the world.

The Big Three

Easily visible from the Bund, three skyscrapers stand out from the Pudong's collection of high rises.

 **Jinmao Tower★★**

(021) 50476688.
www.jinmao88.com.

This tower at 88 Century Avenue (Shiji Dadao) is indeed most striking. Completed in 1998, Jinmao reaches 88 stories in height—it's no mystery that 8 is associated with good fortune in Chinese culture. Modelled on the Kaifeng pagoda in China's Henan Province, it radiates with vermilion flashes at sunset. Inside, the decor is lavish. The last 30 floors, which belong to the **Grand Hyatt Hotel** *(see HOTELS),* center on a gigantic **atrium★** rising from the 53rd floor. Have a drink on the 87th floor at Cloud 9, perhaps the world's highest bar *(see NIGHTLIFE).*

World Financial Center★★

Open daily 8am–11pm (last admission 10pm). 100–150 yuans depending on the floor you want to access. www.swfc-observatory.com.

A key project in the restructuring of the central business district, the World Financial Center was financed by a Japanese-American consortium. Its creation was a tumultuous one: first the Asian

> **Touring Tip**
> To get a good overview of the Pudong, don't miss the walk alongside the Huangpu River on the Pudong's promenade called Binjiang Dadao, especially at dusk.

financial crash in 1997 postponed construction; then its design met with controversy. The top of the tower should have included a circular opening, but it reminded some people of the Japanese imperial flag. Eventually it was changed to a trapezium-like opening, but the entire tower evokes, to some onlookers, a giant bottle opener 101 floors tall. The **view★★★** from the observatory is breathtaking, especially when

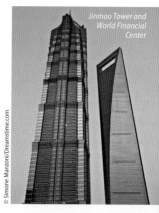

Jinmao Tower and World Financial Center

© Simone Manzoni/Dreamstime.com

Pearl of the Orient Tower

© Martha Bayona/iStockphoto.com

Brussels and the Television Tower in Berlin. A Tinkertoy-like assembly of concrete tubes and glass globes, the tower was built for TV and radio broadcasting purposes. The tower boasts 11 spheres, the largest of which has a diameter of 164ft. There are 15 levels for observation; the highest sits at 1,148ft. On the third floor, the 360-degree **view**★★ extends to the horizon. In the basement, the **Shanghai History Museum**★ *(see MUSEUMS)* offers a lively review of the city's past, with full-size reconstructions of 19C streets.

you step onto the glass floor of the skywalk.

Pearl of the Orient Tower★

Open daily 8am–9:30pm. 50 yuans, access to 2nd floor; 100 yuans, access to three floors and museum. (021) 58791888. www.opg.cn.

Once provocative, the futuristic design of this 1,535ft tower (1995) was inspired by the Atomium in

The Short List

While not anywhere near as tall as the "Big Three" towers, these three attractions won't leave you short on amusement.

Lujiazui Development Showroom★

Open daily 9am–8pm. 5 yuans. (021) 58879964.

The remnants of the old Pudong are preserved in three courtyards

---

Choose Your Crossing

How many ways can you get to the Pudong? Five, but not on foot: the **Yangpu Bridge** (1993) on the north side and the **Nanpu Bridge** (1991) to the south are too far to walk to the Pudong from the city center.

◆ The **Bund Tunnel** under the Huangpu River is the most unusal passage *(open daily 9am–10:30pm, in winter 9:30pm; 30 yuans).* Inside, some 2,132ft of flashing lights, laser rays and holograms entertain passengers. Children will love it, even if the ride is a short one.

◆ **Ferries** depart south of the Bund *(Zhongshan Dong Er Lu near Fang Bang Zhong Lu),* arriving at the south end of Binjiang Dadao in the Pudong.

◆ **Buses** 584, 3 & 4 go to Jinmao Tower from near Shanghai Museum.

◆ The **Metro** is the fastest crossing. Although Line 4 goes to the Pudong, it's best to take Line 2 from People's Square to the Lujiazui station or the Science & Technology Museum station.

◆ A **taxi** is a rather expensive way to get to the Pudong; be sure to avoid the morning rush hour (7:30am–9:30am).

THE PUDONG

MUST SEE

of a remarkable mansion (1917). The first rooms are furnished with Art Deco and Chinese classical furniture; additional rooms exhibit looms, old fishing equipment and photographs of the neighborhood taken every year since 1992.

Shanghai Oriental Art Centre★

Open daily 9am–8pm.
www.shoac.com.cn.

Shaped like a blooming orchid, this center (2005) is dedicated solely to music. Inside its three main round buildings are a 2,000-seat auditorium, a space for operas and a concert hall *(see NIGHTLIFE).*

Science & Technology Museum★

Open Tue–Sun 9am–5:15pm (last admission 3:30pm). 60 yuans. (021) 68622000/6888. www.sstm.org.cn.

Opened in 2001, this huge museum offers a comprehensive introduction to scientific advances largely by way of interactive exhibits that appeal especially to children *(see MUSEUMS).*

The Fast Track

Speed is essential at the two sights below: one in physical movement, the other in its transactions.

Maglev Train★

Inaugurated in 2003, the world's first commercial magnetic levitation train can achieve a maximum speed of 268mph. The train transports passengers from and to the Pudong airport, a distance of 18mi, in only 7 minutes. At the Longyang station, an esplanade was built so that the public can observe the dazzling acceleration of the train after it departs the station.

Shanghai Stock Exchange

Not open to the public. Surrounded by the towering headquarters of Chinese and international firms, the stock exchange has settled within a striking structure of glass and metal. Initially housed in a room in the Astor House in 1990, it has become the most important stock exchange in the country, apart from Hong Kong's exchange. In the transaction area, an average of 60 million orders a day, or 15,000 a second, are executed.

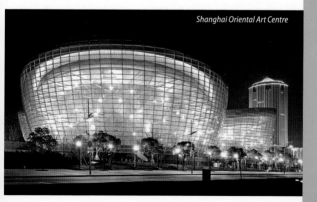

Shanghai Oriental Art Centre

XUJIAHUI

Beyond the border of the Former French Concession, the western part of Shanghai constitutes a different type of hustle and bustle than that of downtown. There are some peaceful spots, though. Longhua Pagoda, the botanical garden and the zoo, in particular, offer tranquil oases away from crowded Nanjing Lu and Huaihai Lu. This suburban corner of the city tucks away some unusual landmarks as well. Get off at Xujiahui Metro station and begin your exploration on foot.

Walking Tour

This self-guided tour encompasses sights within walking distance of the Xujiahui metro station, your place to begin. To the northeast stretches Xujiahui Park, and to the northwest, Jiaotong University extends over a spacious campus. This tour, however, moves to points south of the station, off Caoxi Bei Lu.

St. Ignatius Cathedral ★ – *158 Puxi Lu. Open Sat 1pm–4pm, Sun 1pm–4:30pm.* Founded by Jesuits, this Gothic cathedral, identifiable by its twin spires, was completed in 1910 *(see PLACES OF WORSHIP)*.

Shanghai Stadium – *Open daily 9am–4:30pm. 20 yuans.* This sports center's 69,000-seat stadium (1997) hosts competitions between Shanghai's two major football (soccer) teams *(see FOR FUN)*. An entire mall and a hotel are housed inside. Some hotel rooms have a view of the stadium.

Unique Hill Studio – *907 Tianyaoqiao Lu (Apartment 301). Open Tue–Sun 1pm–6pm. (021) 54104815.* East of the stadium, you will find the studio of Mr. Jiang. His gallery contains an important collection of old advertisements. Some show pretty Shanghai ladies wearing the side-slit dress called the *cheongsam* (*qipao* in Mandarin) or Marilyn Monroe with Chinese features, or a Chinese woman riding a motorcycle. He will also show you his large collection of images, including the Concessions photographed from the sky.

Statue at Longhua Revolutionary Martyrs' Cemetery

Longhua Revolutionary Martyrs' Cemetery★ –

Open daily 6:30am–5pm. Memorial: Open Tue–Sun 9am–4:30pm. www.slmmm.com. South of the studio, you will pass this public space. Behind the graveyard, filled with graves displaying the photographs of the martyrs, stands the striking pyramidal memorial. The park is embellished with huge, patriotic **sculptures**★ that show combative and determined faces.

Longhua Temple and Pagoda★

– *Temple open daily 7am–4:30pm. 10 yuans. The pagoda is closed to the public.* On the outskirts of the cemetery, be sure to glimpse the exterior of the pagoda and take time to see the inside of this ancient Buddhist temple *(see PLACES OF WORSHIP)*.

Outlying Sights

Botanical Garden★

Open daily 7am–5pm. (021) 54363460. www.shbg.org. 15 yuans.

See PARKS AND GARDENS. Created in 1974, this far-flung, 197-acre preserve features several gardens, including the famous Bonsai garden. It's out of the way, yes, but it's also a quiet sanctuary of beauty.

South Railway Station★

The new South Railway Station (2005) was designed by the French architectural firm AREP. It's the first circular station in the world, and reminds some people of a space ship. The round roof is comprised of radiating aluminum blades that let in lots of light to the various levels of the station, giving it a clean, spacious appearance.

Shanghai Zoo★

Open Apr–Sept daily 6:30am–5:30pm. Mar and Oct daily 7am–5:30pm. Nov–Feb daily 7am–5pm. 30 yuans. (021) 62687775.

Opened in 1954, the zoo was renovated a few years ago. It covers 173 acres and hosts 6,000 animals of nearly 600 different species *(see FOR KIDS)*.

Soong Ching Ling Memorial Residence

Open daily 9am–4:30pm. 20 yuans. Mausoleum: daily 8:30–5pm. 5 yuans. (021) 64747183 or 62783104 (mausoleum). www.shsoong-chingling.com.

At the edge of the Former French Concession sits the residence of **Soong Ching Ling** (Song Qingling in the official Pinyin translation in the People's Republic of China), founder of the Chinese Human Rights League, president of the Women's League and widow of Sun Yat-sen). She lived here from 1948 until 1963 before retiring to Beijing. Unlike her two sisters— one married to Chiang Kai-shek, the other one to the rich banker Kung—she joined Mao Zedong, who, she believed, was perpetuating the ideals of her deceased husband (1925). She kept on promoting his cause inside and outside China, and became vice president of the People's Republic of China in 1949, and honorary president in 1981.

The adjacent **museum** tells her incredible story in a simple manner. The most famous Chinese woman of the 20C rests in a **mausoleum** alongside her ancestors.

PLACES OF WORSHIP

Despite being in a country that officially espouses atheism, Shanghai has many temples as well as several mosques, synagogues and cathedrals. During Shanghai's religious festivals, the temples are the centers of celebrations in which centuries-old traditions are practiced and revered. Most sanctuaries are open to the public, and visitors are welcome, especially if respectful and appropriately attired.

Sample Shanghai's Temples

Confucius Temple★

See DISTRICTS, Old Town. 215 Wenmiao Lu. Open Mon–Sat 9am–5pm, Sun 7:30am–4pm. 10 yuans. (021) 63779101/1815. www.confuciantemple.com.

Even though Confucianism is not a religion but a philosophy, temples dedicated to **Confucius** (551–479 BC) rise all over the country. They are places for meditation and inner reflection. The Shanghai Confucius Temple is the city's only such remaining temple. Impressive for its size and the tranquillity found within its

Fast Fact

Just in front of the main gate of the Confucius Temple, two trees are tied with red ribbons hung there by students as vows to achieve success in their studies.

walls, it is also referred to as the "Temple of Literature" *(wen miao)* for the man who was a master of letters *(see Sidebar on next page)*. It was reconstructed in the 19C after an 1855 uprising against the imperial regime.
At the rear of the first courtyard, the second courtyard brings into view the **Hall of Great**

Confucius Temple

Reclining Buddha statue at Jade Buddha Temple

Achievements, dedicated to the Master: it holds the Confucius tablet, the only evocation of him in the sanctuary, which otherwise has no other references to him.

Jade Buddha Temple★

West of People's Square, at the intersection of Anyuan Lu and Jiangning Lu. Open daily 8am–5pm. 5 yuans; additional 10 yuans to see Sitting Jade Buddha statue. www.yufotemple.com.

Recognizable by its ochre-colored walls and the curved roofs of the Song dynasty style, this temple (1924) is famous for two jade Buddha statues. Brought from Burma in the 19C, they were both carved from a single stone. The first statue represents a reclining Buddha draped in delicately carved clothing. His face has a beatific smile at the moment of death. Made of creamy white jade, the sitting Buddha is nearly 6.5ft tall and weighs several tons *(extra fee of 10 yuans to view)*.

Confucius and Confucianism

Confucius (551–479 BC) was a philosopher whose teachings have greatly influenced the culture and politics of China and other Asian countries. The name translates as "Master Kong," his formal name being Kong Qiu. To his followers, he is the master teacher who inspired them to ponder life and study the world around them. **Confucianism** is a philosophy based on his teachings, but it has evolved through the contributions of other thinkers. Basically, man cannot think or act in isolation. The concept of "ren," or humanity, is key. To achieve peace, man must act in the world by actively respecting others. The Chinese man is always identified within a social and political hierarchy that includes his family (immediate and ancestral) and the governing state. Virtuous behavior should govern mankind, eliminating the need for strict rules. Sound morals should be the qualification for authority, not lineage.

Longhua Temple and Pagoda★

See DISTRICTS, Xujiahui.
2853 Longhua Lu. Temple open
daily 7am–4:30pm. 10 yuans.
The pagoda is closed to the public.

Founded in AD 242, this Buddhist temple got its name and its current architectural style in the 15C. Notice the curved roofs typical of the Southern Song period. Rebuilt between 1875 and 1899 after multiple uprisings, the temple is distinguished by a seven-tiered **pagoda**. Behind the door with five arches, the sanctuary was designed by the Buddhist Zen sect, and combines seven temples and courtyards adorned with pine and magnolia trees. It hosts an important community of monks.
In the **Thousand Buddhas Room**, you can listen to the monks singing in the room next door. This favorite sanctuary of the Shanghainese Buddhists has been protected from the rapid modernization of the city. New buildings around it show off traditionally designed façades.

Japanese Buddhist Temple

Map p37. 455 Zhapu Lu, north of the Suzhou Creek.

During the first half of the 20C, the Japanese comprised the largest foreign population in China. Some 30,000 Japanese residents lived in the Hongkou district of Shanghai, north of the Bund (across Suzhou Creek) and located within the perimeters of the international concession. They had their own institutions, facilities and sanctuaries, such as this temple (1931), built by the Japanese architect Okano Shigehisa.
On the façade, designed with a half-moon inset, be sure to admire the geometrical, animal and vegetable **bas-reliefs**.

Jing'an Temple

Map p46. 1686–1688 Nanjing Xi Lu. Open daily 7:30am–5pm. 10 yuans.

The original temple was founded in AD 247 on the banks of Suzhou Creek, but moved here in 1216. During its most recent renovation, from 2002 to 2004, the structure lost all of its former architectural features. In the pre-1949 Shanghai era, it become very popular and was named the **Bubbling Well Temple** at the time, due to the natural spring that stood at the crossroads of Nanjing Xi Lu and Wanhangdu Lu.
Serving an international as well as a Chinese population as it does, this temple, like the city's other houses of worship, is a lively place of devotion, fellowship and learning.

Pagoda of Longhua Temple

© Benjamin Mercer/Fotolia.com

MUST SEE

Temple of the City God

Map p51. 249 Fang Bang Lu.
Open daily 8:30am–4:30pm. (021)
63284494. www.shchm.org.

Rising just south of the Yu Garden,
this Taoist temple is a popular tourist attraction. In the tumult of the
bazaar, worshippers gather in front
of the temple's gate, watched by
passers-by pressed against the
fence. You might catch a glimpse
of the statue of Guo Guang, a
famous general from the Han dynasty. The **Hall of the City God** is
hidden in the backyard. Qin Yubo,
the protector of Shanghai, was an
administrator of the East Sea during the Yuan dynasty (1276–1368).
Next to him stand **Guanyin**, the
goddess of Mercy; and the god
of Health, who is particularly
worshipped at this temple.

Marvel at a Mosque

Mosque of the Small
Peaches Garden★

See DISTRICTS, Old Town. 52
Xiaotaoyuan Jie. Open daily
7am–6pm. (021) 63775442.

Thanks to the donations of its
followers, this mosque was
constructed beginning in 1925.
The symbolic date is written on
the façade: 1343, in the Islamic
calendar. In the inner courtyard,
bordered by buildings used daily,
rises the **prayer hall**, its ceiling
filled with domes. In the center of
the hall hangs the **Islamic flag**,
with its crescent moon.

Mosque of Fuyou Lu

See DISTRICTS, Old Town. 578 Fuyou
Lu. Open daily. (021) 63282135.

A discrete minaret marks this 1870
mosque, which sits in the center
of a tiny courtyard. The two first
rooms are packed with tables and
chairs in typical Chinese style.
The **prayer room** lies in the back.
Chinese and Arabic calligraphies
hang on the walls.

See a Synagogue

Shanghai's first Jewish immigrants
arrived in the early 19C and built
several synagogues. One of the
largest is now a museum.

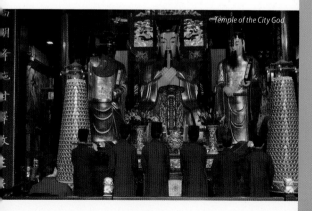
Temple of the City God

Ohel Moishe Synagogue★

Map Inside Front Cover.
62 Changyang Lu, Hongkou. Open
daily 9am–4pm. (021) 65415008.
50 yuans. At the memorial you
will be given a map of the former
Jewish ghetto.

The former Ohel Moishe Synagogue was completed in 1927 by a Jewish community from Vladivostok, Russia—which grew to some 10,000 members at one point. During your visit, the tour guide details the history of this sanctuary. On the ground floor, the small room where worshipers used to gather features photographs of Shanghai's other synagogues (at one time there were seven); the largest and most beautiful of them was Beth Aharon Synagogue, demolished in 1985. A **memorial** to the Jewish refugees who swelled this part of Shanghai during World War II occupies the first floor. A documentary, several exhibits and a series of illustrated books explain daily life in the former Jewish ghetto. In the attic, a room where a Jewish family lived has been reconstructed. In the old brick *lilongs* in the back streets of the ghetto, some Jewish families still dwell today. Here and there a Star of David can be seen on the door frames, such as at No. 54 Chusan Lu. In nearby **Huoshan Park** *(see PARKS AND GARDENS)*, a plaque commemorating Shanghai's Jewish immigrants was dedicated in 1994 by Israel's then-prime minister Yitzhak Rabin.

Check Out the Churches

Shanghai has a number of Christian churches, both Catholic and Protestant.

St. Ignatius Cathedral★

See DISTRICTS, Xujiahui.
158 Puxi Lu. Open Sat 1pm–4pm,
Sun 1pm–4:30pm.

Founded by French Jesuits in 1847, the St. Ignatius Cathedral, also known as Xujiahui Cathedral, was erected between 1904 and 1910 in the French Gothic style: it is adorned with gargoyles and a

---

Religious Festivals

Qing Ming Jie: Celebrated in the spring (usually early April), this day is also known as "tomb sweeping day." The Chinese honor the memory of their ancestors by cleaning their graves, adorning them with flowers and leaving gifts of food.

Longhua Temple Fair: For two weeks in April, the Longhua Temple is the site of Buddhist ceremonies as well as Chinese opera, a parade and other celebratory activities.

Birthday of Guanyin: This festival in March is a celebration of the birthday of Guanyin, the goddess of Mercy. Followers and onlookers attend ceremonies at Buddhist temples throughout the city.

Confucius' Birthday: The one remaining Confucius Temple in Shanghai, as well as Confucius temples across China, are the scene of ceremonies in honor of the great scholar. Adherents typically don traditional costumes, perform dances and play music on ancient instruments.

Religion in Shanghai

Three major streams of thought are practiced: Confucianism, Taoism, and Buddhism. A philosophical belief system, **Confucianism** stresses moral and ethical leadership, rather than laws and punishment, to establish order in society. It calls upon heads of family and heads of state to embody the cardinal virtues of altruism, humanity, loyalty and respect, thereby inspiring loyalty and order in their followers. **Taoism** (or Daoism) emphasizes passive meditation, or non-action *(wu wei)* as the principal means of achieving order through alignment with the Tao (or Dao), the guiding force of reality. The natural universe and all things in it flow from the Tao; spiritual and societal order result from the harmony and balance of opposing natural forces. **Buddhism**, which like Taoism spawned numerous schools of interpretation, teaches that all human suffering arises from the desire for pleasure and material well-being; the only way to achieve peace (nirvana) is to rid oneself of desires by following an eightfold path to Enlightenment. Christianity, Islam and Judaism are also represented in the religious life of the city.

St. Ignatius Cathedral

© claudiozacc/Fotolia.com

American Church of Hongde

Map Inside Front Cover. 59 Duolun Jie. Services every Sunday at 7:30am and 9:30am.

Among the red roofs of this Hongkou neighborhood south of Lu Xun Park, the Chinese-tiled roof of this church (1928) is easily recognized. The **bell tower** was constructed in the Chinese style as well. In fact, the entire edifice resembles a Chinese temple, even though it is a Christian church, built in the memory of an American missionary.

Holy Trinity Church

Map p37. 201 Jiujiang Lu, west of the Bund. Under renovation.

The oldest Anglican church in Shanghai, this Protestant church was built in the Gothic Revival style in 1869 by English architect Sir George Gilbert Scott. Because of its handsome redbrick exterior, it is sometimes nicknamed "the Red Church."

rose window and flanked by two 164ft-high towers. Its twin spires were destroyed at the beginning of the Cultural Revolution (1966), but rebuilt in 1985. The overseers of this Roman Catholic church keep up with the times; television screens have even found a place in the nave. However, the new headquarters of the archbishopric recently built next door makes the church look somewhat outmoded by comparison.

PARKS AND GARDENS

Although Shanghai is rapidly filling its land base with modern buildings and paved streets, a few oases of green remain in this densely populated city. Such reserves of nature and beauty are essential as a counterpoint to the fast pace of urban living. More than any other ancient site, Yu Garden is synonymous with the splendor of Shanghai, attracting visitors the world over. Many other parks dot the metropolis, most of them free. Do as the locals do in these parks: stroll the tree-shaded promenades, sit quietly by a pond, try some tai chi moves, or even fly a kite. Here are a few green spaces not to be missed.

Yu Garden★★

See DISTRICTS, Old Town.
Open daily 8:30am–5:30pm (last admission 5pm). Jul–Aug and Dec–Mar 30 yuans. Rest of the year 40 yuans. (021) 63282465.
www.yugarden.com.cn.

Yu Garden not only is a surprising 5-acre haven of peace and tranquillity in the heart of one of the most populous and fast-paced districts of the city; it also ranks as one of the most attractive classical gardens in all of China. It is the only remaining historical landmark in Shanghai—and is often compared to its prestigious neighbors, the cities of Suzhou and Hangzhou *(see EXCURSIONS)*. Laid out in 1578 by the former governor of Sichuan Province for his father, the garden has survived the transformations of the vicinity, and even today's crowds of tour-bus passengers.

Composed of several waterside courtyards linked by different shaped openings, the garden is a labyrinth of bridges, rock gardens, pavilions, grottoes, and ponds sprouting lotus or stocked with carp. A brook runs through it, adding a sense of unity. The vegetation is part of the magic of the place, with 100-year-old gingko trees, magnolia trees and bonsais.

Yu Garden

Inside the greenhouse, Shanghai Botanical Garden

Botanical Garden★

See DISTRICTS, Xujiahui. Open daily 7am–5pm. 15 yuans. Additional 7 yuans for bonsai garden; 30 yuans for greenhouse, bonsai and 2 other gardens. (021) 54363460. www.shbg.org.

Created in 1974, this far-flung garden, spread over more than 197 acres in the southwest part of the city, is filled with as many as 3,000 different plants. These plants are organized into several categories: medicinal herbs, bamboos, conifers, azaleas, roses and so on.

One of China's most famous, the **bonsai garden★** shelters many species of the miniature trees grown in pots. Some of these trees are almost 200 years old. In addition there are rhododendron and rose gardens, a bamboo area, an herb garden and an orchid garden, as well as demonstration areas. Well worth a visit, the large **greenhouse** has a maze of gateways and lifts that allow the visitor to observe the vegetation from several levels.

Fuxing Park★

See DISTRICTS, Former French Concession. 2 Gaolan Lu. Open daily 5am–9pm (6am–6pm in winter).

Built by the French in 1909, this park is still a popular place for a stroll on the central green amid century-old plane trees and in the rose garden. The park is a hive of human activity: early morning tai chi, afternoon mah-jong, day-long chess and Go games, and occasional ballroom dancing and musical performances. A playground area appeals to children.

Chorus practice at Fuxing Park

David Shen Kai/Apa Publications

PARKS AND GARDENS

Century Park

See DISTRICTS, Pudong. 1001 Jinxiu Lu. Open daily 6am–6pm. 10 yuans. (021) 68565340. www.centurypark.com.cn.

The largest green space in the city covers some 346 acres. Designed by French architect Jean-Marie Charpentier as an **eco-park**, it begins at the east end of Century Avenue in the Pudong, next to the Science & Technology Museum. Families are particularly drawn to the park, since its amusement park, with bumper cars and other rides, is a big draw for children. Pedal and row boats for the park's large lake can be rented, as well as tandem bicycles. The park is a hub for **kite flying**, and there are usually kite-sellers on the premises. Paths have been paved, attracting in-line skaters, and a 9-hole golf course is open to the public. The park is a regular venue for sporting events such as the annual Terry Fox Run as well as other large-scale celebrations.

Huoshan Park

Map Inside Front Cover. Huoshan Lu, Hongkou. Open daily 6am–6pm.

North of the Pudong, in the Hongkou district—the former Jewish quarter of Shanghai—the diminutive, well-maintained Huoshan Park preserves a plaque commemorating the time between 1937 and 1941, when the quarter was the "designated area for stateless refugees." It refers to the Jewish immigrants who lived in Hongkou as refugees during World War II *(see Ohel Moishe Synagogue)*. The park is popular with senior citizens, exercising with fans in hand.

Lu Xun Park

Map Inside Front Cover. In Hongkou. Open daily 5am–7pm.

Join a group of adherents of tai chi for morning exercises beginning at 5am *(until 9 or 10am)* in this park. (Be sure to ask permission of the leader first and possibly pay a fee, though generally it is free). Formerly known as Hongkou Park, Lu Xun Park is a memorial

Stone and flowers in Century Park

Dance practice at Lu Xun Park

David Shen Kai/Apa Publications

style on a U-shaped peninsula of land along a 3,280ft stretch of flowing water. Opened in mid-2004, the 21-acre park is adorned with traditional and modern sculpture and planted with some 10,000 bamboo trees. Surprisingly, there are drink dispensers everywhere in the park.

If you walk farther on Aomen Lu, you will see a gigantic factory: the Shanghai Textile Mill Number 2.

People's Park

See DISTRICTS, People's Square. Open daily 9am–10pm in summer (9am–9:30pm in winter).

to writer **Lu Xun** (1881–1936), who is considered the founder of modern Chinese literature. The park is a lovely large green space with flower plantings, lots of trees, boating lakes, and waterways draped with willow trees. It holds the mausoleum of Lu Xun, a statue of the writer and a small **museum** *(see MUSEUMS)* that displays his works. His **residence** is preserved in the vicinity *(9 New Dalu Village, Shanyin Lu; open 9am–4pm; 8 yuans)*, and along nearby Duolun Lu, his statue stands among other writers such as Guo Moruo and Ye Shentao.

Mengqing Park

Map Inside Front Cover. 66 Yi Chang Lu. Open daily 5:30am–9pm in summer (6am–7:30pm in winter).

Constructed at an elbow bend of Suzhou Creek a few blocks north of the Jade Buddha Temple, this park features an impressive view of the high-rise residences that face it on the other side of the creek. It is designed in a romantic Chinese

Bisected by the broad People's Avenue, this spacious urban park—monumental in scale—has two sections: the lawns, fountains and flowerbeds of the **south park** around the immense Shanghai Museum are beloved by walkers; joggers and cyclists also use the wide paved avenue, which is neatly bordered by hedges and rows of trees. All around, the open sky is punctuated with stratosphere-hugging skyscrapers. Less tall but equally visible are the modernist Grand Theatre and the rather severe-looking city hall.

The **north park**, the setting for the Museum of Contemporary Art Shanghai, or MoCA Shanghai *(see DISTRICTS, People's Square)*, is more of a closed-in space that is visited mostly by the park regulars, the game fans who play chess and Go under the plane trees in front of the pond. From this section of the park, you will get the best **view★★** of landmark high rises that overshadow the square, such as Tomorrow Square and the Park Hotel.

PARKS AND GARDENS

67

MUSEUMS

In a city that is rapidly losing its past to bulldozers and wrecking balls, Shanghai's museums, both private and government-run, are important repositories of all things old. To do justice to the enormous Shanghai Museum, reserve at least one day for a visit, with a lengthy break for lunch. Another two days should be sufficient for the other People's Square museums as well as those in the Bund and the Pudong. But don't miss the art, both old and new, in the Shanghai Art Museum and in MoCA Shanghai *(for description of MoCA, see DISTRICTS, People's Square).*

Shanghai Museum★★★

See DISTRICTS, People's Square. South section, People's Park. Open daily 9am–5pm. Free admission, except for special exhibits. English audio guide 20 yuans. (021) 6372 3500. www.shanghaimuseum.net.

World-famous for its collections of bronzes, ceramics and paintings, the Shanghai Museum possesses 120,000 **artifacts** covering four millennia. It is housed in a building (1994) resembling a *ding*, a traditional cooking container. The design was inspired by Chinese cosmogony: a square base symbolizing the earth, topped by a round roof symbolic of the sky.

The museum has 11 galleries and 3 halls for temporary exhibits.

Collection Highlights

If you like bronzes, make a beeline to the **bronze collection★★★** (18C BC–AD 3C), which showcases some remarkable works decorated with patterns of great variety and precision. Shaped in splendid round and harmonious forms, these bronzes were mainly used as ritualistic containers for wine, rice or meat. From the Shang dynasty on (17C–11C BC), the slender dragon has been favored as a pattern, along with the phoenix. Note in particular the one on the **gu**, an elongated wine cup without handles and a mouth larger than the base. The most delicate inscriptions were carved during the Spring and Autumn period (8C–5C BC) and the Warring States period (5C–3C BC): at this

Shanghai Museum

time, geometrical patterns were combined with figurative bas-reliefs.

The **ceramics collection★★** has some of the oldest works in the museum. Be sure to see the **tripods** from the Longshan Civilization, which flourished in the Yellow River Basin between 2400 and 2000 BC. It was in the Yangtze Basin during the Shang dynasty that conditions were the most favorable for the creation of the world's first china. This period is qualified as the proto-china period, since techniques were not fully mastered at the time. During the Tang dynasty (AD 618–907), **tricolored ceramics** (green, orangish-yellow, and blue) featured a great diversity of animal or human shapes.

A few centuries later, the Southern Song dynasty (AD 1127–1279) developed a very plain style, in which celadon was decorated with gracious vegetal patterns. The most beautiful examples were found in Hangzhou *(see EXCURSIONS)*. Residents of the city of Jingdezhen, in Jiangxi Province (southwest of Shanghai), were masters in creating chinaware until the 15C, first with porcelain that was monochrome, but later with a large variety of patterns and colors. You will see some beautiful

David Shen Kai/Apa Publications

Bronze ritual vessel

examples of bichrome china from the Ming dynasty (1368–1644), as well as some works (17C) adorned with landscapes.

Thanks to lighting that reveals the details of the scrolls, the **paintings gallery★★★** presents exquisite works from the Huadong School of Eastern China, inspired by nature and mastered by scholars. Some of the exhibits date back to the Tang dynasty (AD 618–907). Admire especially the painting of Tang dynasty artist **Sun Wei** showing four sages, or scholars, of the Western Jin dynasty (3C–4C), each seated in a different position.

The Southern Song dynasty's emperors, who lived in Hangzhou *(see EXCURSIONS)*, were also great painters, especially **Zhao Ji** (AD 1083–1135) who painted *Willow, Crows, Reed and Wild Geese*, a scene focusing on birds, a favorite subject of Chinese paintings.

MUSEUMS

During the Yuan dynasty (1276 – 1368), **Ni Zhan** (1301–1374), born in Wuxi (near Suzhou) and one of the four great masters of his time, painted *Clear Autumn Day in Yuzhuang*, in which he gave great importance to the void. The School of Suzhou dominated the Ming period (1368–1644) with masters like **Wen Zhengming** (1470–1559); **Tang Yin** (1470–1523), who used colored ink and detailed all the shadows in his paintings; and **Shen Zhou** (1427–1509), who revealed his admiration for the mountains in his painting *Encounter with an Old Friend in the Autumn Workshop*. Finally, during the Qing dynasty lived excellent painters like **Lan Ying** (1585–1664), with his romantic *Autumn Birds Braving the Cold* and **Mei Qing** (1623–1697), a great figure of the School of the Yellow Mountains, where he went to make paintings that are full of rocks, mists and clouds.

Minority Nationalities Art Gallery

David Shen Kai/Apa Publications

Other Collections

In the **Minority Nationalities Art Gallery**, the museum showcases a superb collection of ethnic dress and adornments, such as fine shell-bead vests and exquisitely embroidered horse-hair and silk shoulder bags. A separate gallery is devoted to the furniture of the Ming and Qing dynasties. And there are galleries solely for the display of Chinese coins, Chinese seals and Chinese calligraphy. Ancient jade and ancient sculpture each have their own gallery.

The Bund Museum★

See DISTRICTS, The Bund.
South Huangpu Park. Open daily 9am–5pm. Free admission.

This slender tower facing Pudong's skyscrapers was part of the former weather station for the French Concession. The building stands out from the rest with its fine Art Deco appearance that features flared pilasters, rounded ironworks and redbrick horizontal bands. Inside, you will find a collection of **vintage photographs** of the Bund, among which one shows a panoramic view in 1923.

Lujiazui Development Showroom★

See DISTRICTS, The Pudong.

Lu Xun Museum★

Map Inside Front Cover. In Lu Xun Park, Hongkou District. Open daily 9am–5pm. 5 yuans.

The writings of **Lu Xun** (1881–1936), a beacon of progressivism and modernity, were a precursor of modern Chinese literature.

MUST SEE

As an essayist, short-story writer and pamphleteer, he criticized the servile attitude of the people in general and the traditional Confucian society in particular. He worked for many newspapers and took part in several Chinese emancipation movements. In Shanghai Lu Xun headed the Chinese League of Left-Wing Writers, founded in 1930. Housed in a vast building of traditional style, the museum relates the historical context of the Chinese revolutions, from the first half of the 20C. Don't miss the superb **wood carving** by the writer himself. The exhibit ends with a collection of foreign publications of Lu Xun, who declared, "'To be a guide for others is all the more difficult, since I do not know myself which way to follow."

Slightly to the north, in **Lu Xun Park★**, Lu Xun has been laid to rest under the shade of two magnolia trees. Local residents go there to relax, do exercises at dawn and embrace their loved ones in front of one of the many ponds.

Museum of Popular Collections★

Map Inside Front Cover. 1551 Zhongshan Nan Lu. Open daily 9am–4pm. Free admission. (021) 63135582.

Situated in the vicinity of Nanpu Bridge, well south of Yu Garden, this museum occupies the former headquarters of the **Guild of the Three Mounts★** (1909), which drew merchants from Fujian Province in southeast China. The guild's hall was built to conform to the architectural

David Shen Kai/Apa Publications

Statue of Lu Xun, Lu Xun Museum

principles of this province, and features an intricately carved **stage** where members put on plays that embodied the life of the guild. Around the courtyard, several rooms exhibit posters, medals, cigarette lighters, pieces of porcelain, tiny shoes used for foot-binding, and other items of daily life from Shanghai's private collections.

Science & Technology Museum★

See DISTRICTS, the Pudong. 2000 Shiji Dadao, the Pudong. Open Tue–Sun 9am–5:15pm (last admission 3:30pm). 60 yuans (additional cost for IMAX and IWERKS). (021) 68622000/6888. www.sstm.org.cn.

With its massive curved, sweeping roof and huge rotating sphere, this modern museum offers visitors a comprehensive overview of recent scientific advances and their daily applications—but makes them fun in the form of hundreds of hands-on exhibits. In total, the museum boasts 12 themed exhibit halls, 6

Science & Technology Museum

new-media theaters, 4 cinemas, 2 art galleries, and a hall for temporary exhibits; there's also a lecture hall, as well as a restaurant and even a bank.

Here you can play chess against a mechanical opponent in the **World of Robots**, ride on an electric swing in **Children's Science Land** and learn about space training in **Space Navigation**, to name just a few of the many activities. The four **movie theaters** *(extra charge)* offer 3D and 4D viewing adventures on topics like outer space, pirates, dinosaurs, and volcanoes and other natural forces.

Shanghai History Museum★

See Map p37. *1 Century Avenue. Open daily 9am–8:30pm. 20 yuans. (021) 52392222.*

Located in the basement of the Pudong's Pearl of the Orient Tower, this fascinating museum offers a lively overview of the city's past, with a special focus on Shanghai when it was the "Paris of the Orient." Galleries depict these seven themes: Ancient Shanghai's Origins; Features of the Urban City; the Open Port; a Street with International Flavor; Traces of the Sea; Architecture; and Transportation. With full-size traditional shops, **reconstructed streets** give visitors a look at 19C Shanghai. They can view former modes of transportation, including a sedan chair, and hear the sounds of the British gunboats that forced Shanghai into a more modern era. There's an **education trail** with animated displays and interactive exhibits.

Bund History Museum

North end, Huangpu Park. Open daily 9am–4:30pm. Free admission. May be closed for renovation.

Located in north Huangpu Park, at the base of the monument to Shanghai's heroes, this museum features an introduction to the city's history, especially the time of the concessions.

Exhibits begin with a photograph showing the signatories to the Treaty of Nanjing, which opened Shanghai's port to international trade. On display are documents on an array of topics such as the economy, the opium trade, trading posts, the city's institutions, and armed forces, including the Indian and Vietnamese contingents. Rare photographs of the bombings and the anti-imperialist demonstrations illustrate aspects of World War II and the Japanese occupation.

Natural History Museum

See Map p36. 260 Yan'an Dong Lu, west of the Bund. Open Tue–Sun 9am–4pm (last admission 3:30pm). 16 yuans. (021) 63213548.

In 1958 the museum settled into this former 1920s cotton exchange. Four **dinosaur skeletons**, a highlight of the exhibits, are housed in the central hall where the cotton transactions were made. Even if the walls of the rooms are faded, the multilevel museum shows off an impressive collection of formaldehyde jars containing human embryos at different growth stages, as well as a variety of preserved amphibians, mammals and birds. The building (1921) was classified by the municipality as an historic landmark, but it was not spared the construction of a suspended highway in close proximity. To admire the structure's dome, you have to cross the avenue.

Shanghai Art Museum

See DISTRICTS, People's Square. 325 Nanjing Xi Lu. Open daily 9am–5pm. 20 yuans. (021) 6359 4542. www.sh-artmuseum.org.cn.

Situated off People's Square in the former clubhouse (1933) for the racetrack that stood where the square is today, this museum houses an excellent collection

Touring Tip

Remember as you tour the Shanghai Art Museum that you are wandering within the walls of the former raceclub. Be sure to look at the guardrails of the main stairs; they are decorated with the heads of horses. Outside, look up at the tall clock tower; the clock used to ring out the start of each race.

of contemporary works. The museum mounts the largest temporary exhibits in Shanghai as well as rotating displays of contemporary art *(few captions in English)*. Temporary exhibits and works of Western artists are displayed on the ground floor. There's a museum shop on the premises and a restaurant on the fifth floor. Every two years, the museum mounts the **Biennale** *(see CALENDAR OF EVENTS)*.

Shanghai Art Museum ↑

Shanghai Municipal Tourism Administration

MUSEUMS

FOR FUN

In addition to its many sightseeing attractions, Shanghai has a wide variety of sporting and fitness activities for your enjoyment. You can feel the sea breeze during a cruise on the Huangpu River, ride a bicycle to the outskirts of the city, play a round of golf, and take kung fu or tai chi lessons.

Activity Sports

Favorite sports in Shanghai are leisurely pursuits such as **golf**, martial arts and table tennis, but **cycling** in the suburbs, as well as **boating** and **swimming** are also possible.

Golf

The latest buzz in the city, golf is *the* activity to practice if one wants to be a fashionable Shanghainese. Several greens have been built out in the vicinity of the Pudong airport, within driving distance of the Pudong's skyscrapers. In exchange for a handful of yuans, visitors have the opportunity to perfect their swings on an 18-hole course. Be sure to phone first to see if and when nonmembers can play.

♦ **Binhai Golf Club** – *Binhai Resort, Baiyunlan Dadao, Pudong. (021) 38001888. www.binhaigolf. com.* Shuttle bus available from Lujiazui, Pudong: next to the MTR Station at 2100 Longyan Lu (Lujiazui station).

♦ **Shanghai Links Golf Country Club** – *1600 Lingbai Lu, Pudong.*

Golf

On all golf courses in Shanghai, players must have caddies. Golf carts are advised since walking the course in 80 to 90 percent humidity is not recommended. If walking, always keep bottled water at hand.

---

(021) 58975899. www.shanghai links.com.cn.

♦ **Tomson Shanghai Pudong Golf Club** – *1 Longdong Avenue, Pudong. (021) 58338888. www.tomson-golf.com.*

Cycling

Given the city's heavy traffic and strict regulations, cycling in Shanghai can be a bit harrowing; however it's quite pleasant to ride a bike in the **Former French Concession** and combine it with a break at a quaint cafe or even do some store hopping. You can also rent bikes in the Pudong's **Century Park** *(see PARKS AND GARDENS)*. Many of the major hotels in Shanghai have bike rental services. The hostels mentioned in this guide rent bikes to paying guests, and URBN hotel offers bike tours to its overnight guests *(see HOTELS)*. Here are places that rent bikes:

♦ **BODHI Adventures** – *Suite 2308, Building 2, 3rd floor, 2918 Zhongshan Bei Lu. (021) 52669013 or cell phone 139 18753119. www.bohdi.com.cn.* BODHI organizes regular weekend biking trips in the Shanghai area. You can rent riding equipment for your own use, as well as a bike, from the club. The one-day bike tour of Shanghai takes in most of the famous city landmarks.

♦ **Giant Bicycle Store** – *743 Jianguo Xi Lu, next to Hengshan Lu,*

Cycling in Century Park

Xujiahui. (021) 64375041. www.shanghaicycling.com. Open daily 9am to 8pm, this store rents brand new bikes. Prices range from about 200 to 1,000 yuans.

◆ **Wolf's Mountain Bike Club** – *138 01953000. wolfs@263.net.* The owner of this club organizes regular weekend bike excursions that take participants out of town. Wolf's can provide any needed accessories for the ride.

Water Sports

Shanghai has a few facilities where you can swim and enjoy other water sports.

 Boating

Boating possibilities are limited within the city, but here are a couple of suggestions:

◆ **Century Park** – *1001 Jinxiu Lu, Pudong. (021) 68565340 (for boat rentals, call 38760588 ext. 218). www.centurypark.com.cn.* Open daily 6am–6pm. 10 yuans. At this immense park near the Science & Technology Museum in the Pudong, you can rent the following boats to use on the park's large lake: Four-person motor boat: 30

yuans/hour. Four-person pedal boat: 30 yuans/hour.

◆ **Shanglong Dragon Boat Club** – *cell phone 136 61447145. www.shanghaidragonboat.com.* This group of rowers from many different countries welcomes visitors for training sessions and barbeques, usually held on weekends. Be sure to take extra clothes to change into after being on the water—it's essential for your comfort.

 Swimming

Public pools are often cheaper but are usually overcrowded. Most of the big hotels have swimming pools, as do Shanghai's many fitness clubs. Some allow access to the public on a paying basis.

◆ **Jing'an Sports Centre** – *151 Kangding Lu, near Jiangning Lu, Jing'an. (021) 62727277.* Open daily 7am–9:30pm. 15–30 yuans. This center has three indoor swimming pools and an area for children.

◆ **Oriental Riverside Hotel** – *2727 Riverside Ave., Pudong. (021) 50370000.* Open daily 6:30am–11:30pm. 80 yuans. Swim with a

David Shen Kai/Apa Publications

Dragon Boat Festival

This festival is historically the most important event of the dragon boating year. Held on the fifth day of the fifth lunar month, it honors the death of Qu Yuan during China's Chou dynasty more than 2,000 years ago. Legend has it that patriotic poet Qu, angry with government corruption, threw himself into the Mei Lo River. To save him, fishermen searched the river, thrashing their oars and beating drums to prevent his being eaten by fish. Today's dragon boat races blend this ancient tradition with a modern, exciting sporting attraction (see CALENDAR OF EVENTS).

view at this hotel's circular pool, enclosed within a glass dome.

Spectator Sports

Shanghai's regular fixtures like soccer (called football in Asia) matches and golf majors are spiced up by Formula 1 Grand Prix and dragon boat races.

Dragon Boat Racing

The annual **Dragon Boat Festival** takes place in Shanghai in May on Suzhou Creek (see CALENDAR OF EVENTS). In September 2009, the Shanghai Dragon Boat Invitational Tournament was held on Xia Yang Lake with 15 teams, both local and international. Many such races are held yearly.

For schedules, contact the Shanghai Sports Bureau, No. 378 Tiyuchang Lu, Qingpu District. (021) 59208539. http://sport.shqp. gov.cn.

♦ **Shanghai Dragon Boat Association** – Room 206, Huakang Building, No.66 Kangping Lu. (021) 64672182.

You can take part in an association **practice session** (50 yuan; Sundays til Dec). Call ahead about bus transportation. Bring a windbreaker, waterproof shoes, a towel, a change of dry clothes, drinking water, sunscreen and a snack, too.

Football

Two international amateur leagues play year-round in the city: the **Shanghai International Football League** (SIFL), founded in 1995, and the **Shanghai Premier League** (SPL), established in 2001. Fielding an average of 17 to 20 teams in two divisions, SIFL plays Saturdays at the Tianma Country Club (season: mid-Sept–early Jun). With an average of 8 teams each year, SPL plays on Sundays on

Shanghai Shenhua at Yuashen Stadium

a grass field in Greencity, in the Pudong (Pudong Jinqiao) *(season: Oct–May)*. Players of both leagues come from many different countries, including the US, Belgium, England, France and Italy.

♦ **Shanghai International Football League** – *www.eteamz.com/sifl*

♦ **Shanghai Premier League** – *www.shanghaipremierleague.net*. The **China Football Association Super League** (CSL) organizes matches in the country at the highest level of competition, attracting teams from various Chinese cities and provinces. Shanghai's famed team, **Shenhua**, plays home matches on weekends primarily at:

♦ **Hongkou Football Stadium** – *No. 444, Dong Jiangwan Lu (beside Lu Xun Park). www.51fb.com*.

Motor Racing
Formula 1 Chinese Grand Prix
Shanghai has its own Formula 1 racing circuit, which stages racing

Shanghai's F1™ Grand Prix

Every October for the past five years, motor-racing fans have flocked to Shanghai's northwest suburb of Anting, some 18 miles from the city's center, for the 3-day Formula 1 Grand Prix races. The track is shaped like a Chinese character that looks like a slanted E. The highest seats on the 10th floor of the steel-and-glass grandstand directly overlook the finish line. Tickets are difficult to come by if not reserved in advance.

No matter when you buy them, good seats are pricey (check to see if credit cards are accepted). You may wish to take the less expensive option: attend a practice session *(see Motor Racing below)*. A bus line runs from Shanghai Stadium to Anting. Contractually, the F1 races of the Shanghai International Circuit are scheduled to end after 2010, unless the contract is renewed. But for the 2010 World Expo, the F1 races will be moved up to April 17 and take place over 18 days. For more information, access www.icsh.sh.cn.

events year-round. In 2010 the Formula 1 Chinese Grand Prix is scheduled for mid-April *(see CALENDAR OF EVENTS)*. Tickets to watch the race cost from 160 to 3,980 yuans (about $23–$568). If you want to experience the excitement of driving on a Formula 1 track, you can book a session at the **Formula 1 Driving Center** *(information: 021 69569545)*: various packages are available—from a 5min to a 20min drive, with an instructor at your side. Prices range from 200 to 2500 yuans (about $30-$350USD). For details, contact the following:

♦ **Formula 1™ Chinese Grand Prix, Shanghai International Circuit** – *2000 Yining Lu, Anting Town, Jiading District (021) 96826999. www.icsh.sh.cn.*

Other Activities

🚣 Cruising the River

One of Shanghai's most popular companies to operate river tours is the **Shanghai Huangpu River Cruise Company** *(see opposite)*. In fact, a number of booths on the Bund sell tickets for different boat tours and various packages, or you can ask at your hotel; there's no need to book in advance. Tour boats depart at the south end of the Bund on a regular basis. En route, depending upon which tour you choose, you may see the river's **confluence★★** with Suzhou Creek, where you'll be treated to the best **view★★★** of the Pudong and the Bund. At this "elbow" of the river, the tour offers a thrilling moment: right in the middle of the maneuver to turn around, the boat drifts slowly outwards, before getting back on course.

Other highlights of the tour are Shanghai's **cable-stayed bridges★**. Inaugurated not long after the launch of Pudong's development plan, the **Nanpu Bridge** and **Yangpu Bridge** are the only ones to cross the Huangpu River in the central part of the city (other passageways are underwater). The river is wide (1,312ft to 1,640ft), hence the bridges must have cable-stayed construction to span such a distance. With a central span of 1,388ft, the Nanpu Bridge (1991) is supported by two towers 492ft tall. Rising 151ft high, the bridge is linked to the main roads of Puxi (the west side), thanks to a double spiral connection. The Yangpu Bridge (1993) has an even longer span at 1,975ft, and its reverse-Y-shaped towers top out at 722ft above the Huangpu River.

♦ **Shanghai Huangpu River Cruise Co.** – *(021) 54106831. www.pjrivercruise.com.* 1hr cruises depart daily 9am–9pm, 2hr cruises between Nanpu and Yangpu bridges depart daily 9am–7pm, and 3.5hr cruises to the confluence of the Yangtze River depart once in the morning and once in the afternoon.

Martial Arts

Tai chi and kung fu are practiced by many Shanghainese, and are often done in parks, plazas and other public places. While in Shanghai, you may wish to take formal lessons, or simply join a crowd as they exercise at dawn (around 5am until 9pm or 10pm) in People's Square, Fuxing Park or Lu Xun Park. Always ask the group's master leader first if you may participate in their session.

Longwu International Kung Fu Center

◆ **Longwu International Kung Fu Center** – *1 Maoming Lu, next to Julu Lu, French Concession. (021) 62871528. www.longwukungfu.com. Open daily 7am–7pm.* This center provides professional lessons in Shaolin-style kung fu, traditional tai chi, tae kwon do, karate, boxing and kick boxing. Classes are taught both in Chinese and English.

Yoga

Practitioners of yoga can also be found throughout Shanghai. Some hotels have group sessions or classes, and there are a few commercial centers that offer lessons.

◆ **Body & Soul Yoga Club** – *470 Shanxi Bei Lu (at Xinzha Lu), Building 12, Jingan. (021) 32180009. www. bodynsoulyoga.com.* This center, about a 3min walk north of Plaza 66, offers small classes in English.

◆ **Y+ Yoga Center** – *No. 202 Hubin Lu, 2nd Floor, Corporate Avenue 2 (off Huangpi Nan Lu near Xintiandi. (021) 63406161. www.yplus.com.cn.* With three locations, this upscale center has 30 full-time instructors

and offers more than 800 yoga courses and workshops a month.

Karaoke

Karaoke is by far the most popular activity at a gathering of friends in China. It doesn't matter if you aren't a soprano or if your vocal skills don't equal those of famous Chinese pop stars like Faye Wong or Andy Lau; everyone is permitted to sing at least one song no matter how bad it may sound.

The most popular of all the karaoke chains in China is Partyworld. It has one of its biggest branches in Shanghai's Fuxing Park. Depending on the number of people and the hour of the day, prices range from around 20 yuans to more than 250 yuans an hour. A free buffet is served after midnight, and there's even a large choice of English songs.

◆ **Partyworld** – *109 Yandang Lu, inside Fuxing Park. (021) 6374 1111. www.cn.cashboxparty.com. Open daily 8am–2am.*

FOR KIDS

Children are most welcome in China. It's a common sight to see adults trying to get the attention of a blond toddler, or parents pushing their own kids to play with the children of newcomers. With the country's one child policy, these "small friends," as they are called by Chinese adults, have become the most treasured members of a family. Shanghai has several attractions that compete for children's attention, including a zoo, an aquarium, amusement parks, and of course the acrobatic shows, which always appeal to a younger audience.

Family Fun

Shanghai Ocean Aquarium★★

1388 Lujiazui Ring Lu, Pudong New Area. Open daily 9am–6pm. 120 yuans, children 80 yuans. (021) 58779988. www.sh-soa.com.

Lying just east of the Pearl of the Orient Tower, this aquarium is one of the largest in the world. It showcases a wide range of Chinese sea creatures, such as the **Yangtze alligator** and the **Chinese giant salamander**. It is home to an amazingly long (1.5ft) **goldfish** named Bruce, after the

kung fu movie star Bruce Lee. At the longest marine tunnel in the world (509ft), admire strange creatures like the Japanese spider crabs or the leafy sea dragon, alongside more commonly known sharks and giant manta rays. Most recently, the aquarium has added peppermint shrimp, garden eels and Hawaiian boxer crabs. Apart from the cold-blooded animals, the Humbolt penguins, in the Polar Zone, are the most fun to watch. **Animal feedings** take place twice a day, between 10am and 11:30am and from 2:40pm to 4:30pm.

Night camp at Shanghai Ocean Aquarium

MUST DO

Pearl of the Orient Tower★

The Pudong. Open daily 8am–9:30pm. Combined tickets: 100 yuans, access to three floors and the museum; 85 yuans, access to the first two floors and the museum; 70 yuans, access to the 2nd floor and the museum. Regular tickets: 50 yuans, access to the 2nd floor; 20 yuans, access to the museum. 50% off for children under 4ft in height. (021) 58791888.

This tower attracts kids like a giant space rocket would. From the upper floors, the **view**★★ is amazing, even though Shanghai now has higher vantage points *(see DISTRICTS, the Pudong).* Younger ones might be even more excited to visit the **Shanghai History Museum**★ in the basement of the tower. Here they'll see a long-gone Shanghai and vehicles like wheelbarrow taxis, sedan chairs and buses that used to throng the streets when the city was known as "Little Suzhou." Life-size reconstructions of shops, a stock exchange and artisan workshops with wax figures hint at the daily life of Shanghai in the early 20C. Don't miss artifacts such as the carved lions that used to guard the entrance to the Hong Kong and Shanghai Bank (HSBC) and the public phones that you can dial to listen to opera.

Science & Technology Museum★

Open Tue–Sun 9am–5:15pm (last admission 3:30pm). 60 yuans, students 45 yuans (additional cost for IMAX and IWERKS). www.sstm.org.cn.

Also see MUSEUMS. This immense museum will especially endear itself to parents who are concerned about their children's education as well as the children themselves, who are usually in need of engaging activities. Just follow the trail and visit the five interactive science halls. Highlights of the visit include exploding **volcanoes** and a tropical **rain forest** on the first floor, and the **robots** and spiders on the second floor. A simulated laboratory was added to the museum so that children can conduct experiments themselves. If you choose to add an IMAX or IWERKS attraction *(extra charge)*, the kids may want to stay here all day.

Shanghai Zoo★

Open Apr–Sept daily 6:30am–5:30pm. Mar and Oct daily 7am–5:30pm. Nov–Feb daily 7am–5pm. 30 yuans. (021) 62687775.

Opened in 1954, this 173-acre zoo hosts 6,000 animals of nearly 600 different species. The **golden fish** are counted among the stars of the zoo: they swim in giant open-air aquariums. Don't miss the Asian elephants, the Przewalski wild horses, the South China tigers, the Japanese cranes—and of course the **giant panda**, king of the animals in China. The Ferris wheel has been there since the opening.

Barbie Shanghai

555 Huaihai Zhong Lu. Open daily. 400 6208181. www.barbieshanghai.com.

Based in a 6-story building lit up with flashy pink neon, the first Barbie shop in Shanghai sells Barbie products and offers activities designed solely for Barbie lovers. Hundreds of different dolls are exhibited here, from Barbie French to Barbie Chinese and Barbie Princess. The highlight is definitely the **Design Center**, where youngsters can create their very own Barbie doll.

Shanghai Yinqixing Indoor Skiing

1835 Qixing Lu, Xinzhuang.
Open daily 9:30am–10:30pm (Fri and Sat until 1am). Weekdays 98 yuans per hour; weekends 118 yuans. Free shuttle bus every hour at Xinzhuang metro station.

Shanghai's residents love this new indoor resort. Yet people who are used to skiing in the Alps or the Colorado Rockies surely won't be thrilled about this artificial slope. Snowboarders might find the snowboard park more challenging. Nevertheless, kids will be delighted to play in the snow when it's 90 degrees outside.

🐼 Wanshang Flower, Bird, Fish and Insect Market

Dongtai Lu. Open daily 8am–5pm.

Puppies, kitten, hamsters and birds: basically any sort of pet can be found here, along with beautiful, handmade birdcages. In the summer, a whole section of the market is dedicated to a pet that the Chinese have bred since the Tang dynasty: crickets. Against the background of their deafening "singing," hundreds and hundreds of crickets are sold here. They are kept in small bamboo or ceramic boxes for the sounds they make.

Wanshang bird market

🐼 Kung Fu Kids

If your children know Bruce Lee, Jackie Chan or Jet Li from the movies, drop them off at one of Shanghai's kung fu centers that organize lessons for children. You can ask for a free trial for your child at a center below:

Longwu International Kung Fu Center

1 Maoming Lu, next to Julu Lu. Open daily 7am–7pm. (021) 62871528. www.longwukungfu.com.

No need to go to Shaolin (Henan Province) to learn the style from the temple that developed the art of kung fu. Coaches here teach kids twice a week on weekends (mornings 10am–11:30am; 600 yuans for one month).

Wuyi Chinese Kung Fu Center

Room 311, 3rd Floor, International Artists' Factory, No. 3, Lane 210, Taikang Lu. Cell phone 137 01685893.

For 600 yuans per month, on Thursdays and Saturdays, this well-known address in the Taikang arts district welcomes children, and adults as well, for kung fu lessons.

Amusement Parks

These two parks are open in summer to offer kid-friendly fun:

Jinjiang Amusement Park

201 Hongmei Lu. Open daily 8:45am –5pm, and summer nights 6pm– 10pm. 80 yuans. (021) 5421 6858 or 54200844 www.jjlysh.com .

It's not state of the art, but this amusement park has a giant Ferris wheel (the newest attraction of the park), a pirate ship and mini roller coasters. Other attractions look slightly dated, but the kids scream for joy while riding anyway.

Dino Beach

78 Xinzhen Lu. Open Jun–early Sept daily: call or go online for hours. 150 yuans, children under 4ft 80 yuans. (021) 64783333. www.64783333.com. Shuttle bus from Xinzhuang metro station (Line 1).

This is the only beach facility available in summer for relief from the suffocating heat of Shanghai, so be prepared for crowds. After putting your towel on the sand, enjoy the many themed **water slides**, the beach and the wave pool, for which tubes can be rented. Absolutely avoid weekends if you want an opportunity to ride the waves.

Acrobats and the Circus

Children of all ages will delight in Chinese acrobats and the circus:

Lyceum Theatre

57 Maoming Nan Lu. (021) 62565544 (tickets).

Acrobatics and Chinese opera are regularly staged under the arched ceilings of this historic theater *(see PERFORMING ARTS).*

Shanghai Centre Theatre

1376 Nanjing Xi Lu. (021) 62798663 or 62797132. www.shanghai acrobats.com.

The **Shanghai Acrobatic Troupe** performs here daily at 7:30pm. It is one of the best known performing groups in the country.

Shanghai Circus World

2266 Gonghexin Lu, Zhabei. (021) 6652 2395. www.circus-world.com.

State-of-the-art acoustics and lighting add a modern twist to the shows here, which include the **Shanghai International Magic Festival and Competition** *(see CALENDAR OF EVENTS).* Situated on the northern outskirts of the city, the venue is reached by metro *(line 1, Shanghai Circus World station).* Shows at 7:30pm *(reservations strongly recommended).*

Chinese acrobats at Shanghai Centre Theatre

David Shen Kai/Apa Publications

BOX OFFICE

PERFORMING ARTS

Shanghai is inching toward the diverse arts and cultural scene one would anticipate for a city of its magnitude. There is much to entertain visitors, especially the popular acrobatic shows, Chinese opera and various musical performances. Shanghai boasts a couple of world-class venues, symphonies, opera troupes and theatrical companies, a ballet and the largest film festival in China. More recently, Broadway and off-Broadway shows are being imported with regularity.

Classical Music and Opera

Shanghai Broadcasting Symphony Orchestra

300 Renmin Dadao, People's Square. (021) 63728702. www.shgtheatre.com.

Now the resident orchestra at the Shanghai Grand Theatre *(see below)*, this orchestra was established in 1996 with the help of the city's cultural bureau. Its repertoire has grown to include operatic works and balletic pieces as well as symphonic scores.

Shanghai Symphony Orchestra

Concert Hall, 105 Hunan Lu. (021) 64375617 (tickets 64333574). www.sh-symphony.com.

The much-respected Shanghai Symphony Orchestra (SSO) had its formal beginnings in 1907. A major force in the history of symphonic music in China, the SSO has given thousands of concerts in the country, and toured both the US and Europe. Check online for the latest concert schedule; in season, the SSO performs at the Shanghai Grand Theatre and other venues as well as in its own hall.

Peking Opera

Chinese Opera

More like a performance of a folk tale on stage, Chinese opera has dwindled in popularity over the past few years. An art form in itself, Peking opera has been performed in Shanghai for more than 100 years; it was once the most popular form of entertainment, especially during Chinese festivals. Spurred by the decline, attempts are being made to revive it. Although performances of full-length operas (which may last more than three hours) are held at conventional theaters, local opera groups aim to make the genre more approachable, especially to international visitors.

Shanghai Opera House

No.10, Lane I00, Changshu Lu. (021) 62491666. www.shanghaiopera. com.cn.

Founded in the mid-1950s, the Shanghai Opera House is a performing arts company dedicated to Western and Chinese (both traditional and contemporary) operas. It stages its productions at various venues in the city such as the Shanghai Grand Theatre and the Shanghai Concert Hall.

Shanghai Oriental Art Centre

425 Dingxiang Lu, Pudong. (021) 38424800. www.shoac.com.cn.

This mammoth state-of-the-art structure was designed by the French architect Paul Andreu to recall the five petals of an orchid. Opened in 2005, the center is the crown jewel of the Pudong's cultural venues. It contains three performance spaces, of which the 1,953-seat concert hall holds China's largest pipe organ.

Conservatory of Music

20 Fenyang Lu via Huaihai Zhong Lu, Former French Concession. (021) 54370137. www.shcmusic.edu.cn.

The public is welcome to attend concerts by students—and sometimes visiting artists—usually held on weekend evenings in this 780-seat campus venue.

Shanghai Concert Hall

523 Yan'an Lu. (021) 63384401. www.culture.sh.cn.

This major venue near the People's Square is one of Shanghai's most historic concert halls. It was built in 1931 in the central part of the city. To reduce increased traffic noise, it was moved 216 feet in late 2002, and later expanded to a capacity of 1,200 seats. The hall has hosted some of the world's top performers and orchestras. Many Shanghai orchestras and local musical groups hold their concerts here.

Chinese Music and Opera

Shanghai National Orchestra

336 Xinhua Lu. (021) 34642122 or 62835288. www.sh-co.com.cn.

Formed in 1952, this is one of the oldest orchestras in the country. Performing at various city venues, some 80 musicians play traditional Chinese instruments such as flutes, drums, gongs and plucked and

Shanghai Grand Theatre

bowed stringed instruments. Concerts are often a medley of popular opera, and musical and folk tunes.

Shanghai Peking Opera Troupe

168 Yueyang Lu.
www.pekingopera.sh.cn.

Annually, this professional company mounts an ambitious schedule of operatic productions of classical Chinese opera. Their colorful performances are usually held at the Yifu Theatre as well as in youth centers, on university campuses, and at other venues in Shanghai. The troupe has toured Europe, and has won prestigious awards.

Theater

Theatrical productions in Shanghai run the gamut from New York touring companies to Shanghainese takes on classic plays. Drama has become more creative in recent years, but the propaganda bureau is always at the ready to check scripts before they take to the stage.

Lyceum Theatre

57 Maoming Lu at Changle Lu, Former French Concession. (021) 62178530. www.culture.sh.cn.

Installed within a lovely building dating to 1931, the Lyceum is the oldest theater in Shanghai. Its programs range from Yue and Peking opera to productions geared toward children.

Getting Tickets

Two useful websites for Shanghai cultural events and ticket sales are www. culture.cn and www.365ttk.cn. You can also go to www.ticketmaster.cn.

MUST DO

Majestic Theatre

66 Jiangning Lu, near Nanjing Xi Lu. (021) 62174409. www.culture.sh.cn.

Another grande dame of the city's theater scene, the Majestic has gained considerable prestige in Asia since it opened in 1941. Its productions center on traditional music and dance as well as Hu opera.

Shanghai Art Theatre

466 Jiangning Lu via Wuding Lu. (021) 62568282. www.culture.sh.cn.

Basing itself in the wing of the Yi Hai Mansion, this cultural complex (2001) occupies the first floor and has a seating capacity of 999. At its disposal are three additional floors for dressing rooms, prop storage, rehearsal rooms, offices and class rooms. Offerings are devoted to classical music, Chinese opera, dance and some avant-garde shows.

Shanghai Centre Theatre

1376 Nanjing Xi Lu, near Xikang Lu, Jing'an. Ticket office (021) 62798663. www.shanghaicentre.com/theatre.

This top-notch venue in the **Port-man Ritz-Carlton Hotel** has plush seating for a capacity audience of 991 people. The theater specializes in Chinese acrobatic shows and musical revues primarily of the Hollywood and Broadway variety. Reservations are recommended.

Shanghai Dramatic Arts Centre

288 Anfu Lu, Former French Concession. (012) 64734567. www.china-drama.com.

This company is China's only national drama group. The art form began to appear only as the country began to modernize, and the center' performers, most of them young, have contributed much to the art form's growth. A full schedule of contemporary drama, Broadway shows and British comedies is offered at the Anfu Lu location.

Shanghai Grand Theatre

300 Renmin Dadao, at corner of Huangpi Bei Lu and People's Square. (012) 63728702. www.shgtheatre.com.

This huge, futuristic-looking structure was designed by French architect Jean-Marie Charpentier and opened in 1998. It has become the city's premier showplace for touring companies and international artists such as cellist Yo-Yo Ma, and is a venue for many of the city's annual arts festivals as well. At night, the lighting of the curved roof's underbelly is a particularly dramatic sight.

Yifu Theatre

701 Fuzhou Lu, near Yunnan Lu. www.tianchan.com. www. culture. sh.cn.

Founded in 1925, Yifu—also known as the Tianchan Peking Opera Centre—is the Carnegie Hall of Chinese opera in the city. Conveniently located near People's Square, it is, without doubt, the favored venue for Shanghai's opera companies; many of China's greatest operatic artists have performed here.

PERFORMING ARTS

SHOPPING

As a major commercial capital of China, Shanghai is a shopper's mecca, attracting residents from all parts of the country as well as tourists and the Shanghainese themselves. Outdoor markets, Western-modelled malls, private and government-owned stores, upscale boutiques, street vendors, museum stores and even hotel gift shops offer a broad shopping experience for the visitor. So get your wallet and enter the fray.

Before You Buy

Opening Hours – Markets are usually open daily from 7am or 8am to about 6pm. Mall hours are generally 10am–10pm every day. Individual stores open from 10am–9pm each day; privately owned boutiques may not open until 11am, and state-run businesses may stay open until 10pm, usually in summer. On weekends the stores are usually the most crowded, especially on Sundays.

Public Conveniences – Shopping malls and department stores have fairly well-maintained facilities.

Bartering

In China, haggling is pretty much expected, except in supermarkets and state-run stores. But be forewarned, the Chinese are masters at negotiating. It's a good idea to have a sense of humor, be patient and keep smiling. Except for certain products like electronics, don't hesitate to bargain for discounts off the suggested retail price. You may be able to secure as much as 30 to 50 percent off an item, but don't wrangle over small amounts. To get an idea of the final prices charged, observe the transactions around you and how much currency changes hand. Above all, deal with only one vendor at a time, ideally when no other vendors are nearby: saving face is extremely important to the Chinese.

Chinese Specialties
Calligraphy

This ancient Chinese art is still practiced in China today. To produce this highly varied style

Silk for sale

MUST DO

of penmanship requires four elements, the "four treasures of the well-read man": paper, ink (in stick form or liquid; the latter may not pass airline security), an ink stone or ink slab, and a brush. Traditional ink colors are purple, black, green and white, although red and blue are now used as well. Brushes vary from large with soft bristles to small with stiff bristles. For beginners, a calligraphy set might make a good gift, or even a calligraphy scroll.

Calligraphy

David Shen Kai/Apa Publications

Ceramics

The manufacture of ceramics is also a very old art in China. Except for celadon, it is a speciality of the city of Hangzhou (see EXCURSIONS), where many stores sell ceramics in all styles (blue and white, the family of pinks, etc.) and in all price ranges. Shanghai has a number of shops selling celadon tea cups, blue and white porcelain and other ceramic wares. The majority of pieces are factory-made; finding a handmade piece is a rarity. Cups, plates, bowls, vases and other serviceware come in a variety of styles, colors and patterns.

Silk

In China—the country where this noblest of all fabrics was invented—silk can be bought at affordable prices, in comparison with prices found in Europe, for example. Hangzhou and Suzhou (see EXCURSIONS) are China's most famous cities for silk production; an immense silk market is held in Hangzhou, while large factories in Suzhou sell their products directly. Shanghai offers many outlets where silk may be purchased, either as fabric (beware of synthetics rather than real silk),

Orient Yourself

For bustle and bargains, head to **Nanjing Dong Lu,** Shanghai's famed shopping street—once the most well-known shopping street in Asia: the pedestrian-only section begins with the No.1 Department Store, where bargains line the ground floor and pricey items are upstairs. Nanjing's western section hosts big names and modern malls. The premier shopping thoroughfare south of Nanjing is **Huaihai Lu,** strung with high-end designer shops. **The Bund** has a monopoly on the luxury market. **Old Town** is home to many lively outdoor markets. For a less frenetic shopping experience, the charming boutiques of the **French Concession** and **Xintiandi's** trendy shops are your best bet, albeit pricey. Across Suzhou Creek, the **Hongkou** district has its own major shopping street, Sichuan Bei Lu, and its own pedestrian-only Duolun Lu, dotted with fun shops.

SHOPPING

or ready-made clothing. Sizes in Shanghai tend to be on the small side, so be sure to try on any garment you intend to buy. Except for some of the larger department stores, sales are almost always final. Custom-made pieces can usually be completed by a tailor in a couple of days to a week after measurements are taken.

Other Purchases

Electronic products are still much less expensive in China, and Shanghai's specialized shopping malls attract thousands of international buyers searching for good bargains. Look for wares that are in their original packaging, or ask to see it. Guarantees made in China will not automatically be valid in the US, so weigh your buying decision carefully before making a purchase. Keep all receipts and the business card of the seller.

Propaganda souvenirs and Mao paraphernalia overflow the flea markets of Shanghai. You will see plenty of copies of Mao Zedong's little red book, Cultural Revolution posters from his years as chairman, and statues in his image, as well as other **Mao memorabilia**.

The world's largest textile producer offers some unbeatable prices on many articles of **clothing**. With its sizable population of fashion-conscious women, Shanghai carries most of the top brand names of couture designers in its shops, but usually with high-end price tags. There are Shanghainese designers to be found, however. Or why not hunt for the perfect *qipao*, the celebrated sleeveless Chinese dress with a side slit, or for a man's shirt with a Mao collar?

Shipping Goods Home

Small shops do not, as a rule, provide shipping services. You will have to use the Chinese postal service, which is generally very reliable. However, in Shanghai and other large cities, antiques shops and furniture stores should be able to ship your bulkiest purchases by air cargo (fast) or by container (slower, but less expensive). Generally speaking, your airplane ticket gives you the right to send

Chairman Mao statues

Dongtai Lu Flea Market

your bulky luggage (more than 44 lbs) by freight with the help of a supplemental air carrier (Air France Cargo liner, Air China Cargo, etc.). You must deposit this luggage, clearly labelled with sender and recipient, in a designated hangar close to the airport two to three days before the departure.

Shanghai Markets

In Shanghai, flea markets, outdoor markets with birds and plants, book marts and night markets are numerous and varied. Usually you will find that the prices are lower, but the quality of the merchandise is also lower.

Here are a few to sample:

Dongtai Lu Flea Market

(see Old Town Map; Liuhekou Lu and Zizhong Lu; open daily 8am–6:30pm) consists of three pedestrian-only streets with antiques stalls and stores, and lots of good deals for buyers willing to negotiate. You'll find Mao statues, ethnic clothing and jewelry, Art Deco lamps, vintage posters, bird cages, lanterns, baskets and more.

Antiques Market *(see Old Town Map; Fang Bang Zhong Lu at the* corner of Henan Nan Lu; open daily 7am–8pm)*, near Yu Garden in Old Town, is similarly touristy like the Dongtai Lu Market. Here you will discover all sorts of treasures such as ethnic Yunnan bags, reproductions of traditional furniture, wrought-iron handles, even doors.

Fabric Market

(168 Dongmen Lu at the corner of Waixiangua Jie; open daily 8:30am–6pm) takes up an immense hall filled with a vast array of silks, cashmere, linens, brocades, cottons and other fabrics for sale at enticing prices. Tailors on

SHOPPING

the premises can custom-make clothing to your size, but be sure to have a photo of the outfit you want and find an interpreter to help make yourself clear.

Bird and Plant Market *(see Old Town Map; 405 Xizang Nan Lu; open daily 8am–6pm)* sits southwest of the Confucius Temple, in Old Town. It's stocked with all manner of animals such as fish, chickens, rabbits and caged birds (parrots, canaries, pigeons, etc.) as well as myriad flowers and plants.

Modern Electronic City *(Xiangyang Lu and Fuxing Zhong Lu)* is an electronics market that offers many good deals. It is located in the middle of the old French Concession. Here you'll find cell phones, MP3 players, webcams, CDs, speakers and more.

Book Market at Confucius Temple *(see Old Town Map; 215 Wenmiao Lu; every Sun 8am–4pm)* is held in the courtyards of the temple dedicated to the master of Chinese thought. Crowds of collectors and book lovers come to hunt for second-hand tomes, magazines, comic books, and encyclopedias. The majority of works are in Chinese, but the market provides an environment that encourages the finding of a true gem in one's own language.

Datong Tea Market *(Datong Lu; open daily 7:30am–2pm)* will be of special interest to connoisseurs of tea. There are hundreds of stalls here where you can taste, before you buy, all types of the beverage in the age-old tradition of the tea ceremony.

Culinary Specialties

Shao Wan Sheng *(414 Nanjing Dong Lu at the corner of Shanxi Lu)* is a specialty shop where one's eyes are attracted to thousands of delicacies such as candies, dried fish, vegetables and fruits, tea and more.

Sanyang Nanhuo *(630 Nanjing Dong Lu)* specializes in the foodstuffs of the seaport city of Ningbo, not far from Shanghai. One such food is rice dumplings called *Ningbo tangyuan*, which are stuffed with a mixture of ground seasame seeds and sugar and wrapped in sticky rice powder.

Yunhong Chopsticks Shop *(387 Nanjing Dong Lu; 021 63220207)* stocks all types, colors and forms of the Chinese eating utensil.

Fashion and Home

Maoming Lu sports a row of shops that sell Chinese-inspired clothing, including the now fashionable-again *qipao* (sleeveless woman's gown with high collar and slitted side). It's the ideal place to have one custom made.

Shanghai Trio *(181 Taicang Lu, near Huangpi Nan Lu, Xintiandi; Showroom: Lane 37, 6 Fuxing Xi Lu; 021 64338901 or 63552974; www. shanghaitrio.com.cn)* showcases the creations of French designer Virginie Fournier. Inside you'll find linens and tablecloths and other accessories for the home, silk bags a children's line of clothing and more. The artisan-made goods combine Asian and Western influences.

Shanghai Tang *(In Jin Jiang Hotel, 59 Maoming Nan Lu; open daily 10am–10pm; 021 54663006; www. shanghaitang.com)* is a Hong

Kong label of high-end, high-priced couture. The international company reinterprets traditional Chinese clothing in pop colors for men, women and kids. There's a line of housewares also.

Shirt Flag (330 Nanchang Lu, near Maoming Lu; 800-820-3710, www.shirtflag.com) is an amusing shop opened by artists who knowledgeably mix the imagery of the Cultural Revolution with contemporary urban themes on their tee-shirts, which are targeted to young buyers.

Suzhou Cobblers (17 Fuzhou Lu; open daily 10:30am–6:30pm; 021 63217087; www.suzhou-cobblers.com) is a pretty shop located steps from the Bund that sells shoes and slippers, handbags and children's clothing, all traditionally styled and of good quality.

210 Taikang Lu (French Concession) is a little lane called the "Art Street," with rows of art galleries and shops tucked into old buildings. At No. 2 sits the **Deke Erh Art Center**, founded by author/photographer Deke Erh. At No. 3 is the **International Artists' Factory**, a building housing clothing shops and home decor boutiques over several floors: among the most interesting are **Artique**, with an assortment of rugs and cashmere goods, **Jooi Design** with items for the home, and **Happiness Is Fashion** for urban wear created by Sylvia Soo.

Cha Gang (70 Yong Fu Lu, 1st floor, French Concession; open Tue–Sun 11am–7pm; 021 64373104; www.chagang.cn) is the groundbreaking boutique of innovator Wang Yi Yang, who, like other contemporary Shanghai designers, views clothing as an art form.

Originating in the province of Jilin, the brand poetically reinterprets traditional Chinese clothing, creatively displayed in his minimalist-styled Shanghai shop.

Rouge Baiser Elise (299-2 Fuxing Xi Lu; 021 64318019; www.rougebaiser-elise.com) is an ultra-stylish boutique that specializes in classic French hand-embroidered bedding and table linens, as well as women's fashions and a line of children's clothing.

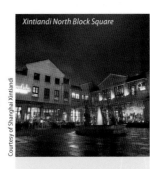
Xintiandi North Block Square

Courtesy of Shanghai Xintiandi

Xintiandi

Frequented mainly by ex-pat residents, tourists and well-to-do Shanghainese, this pedestrian-only neighborhood mixes restored *shikumen (see box in DISTRICTS)* and new buildings along tree-shaded lanes. Fashionable boutiques, art galleries, bookshops, Western-style bars, and cafes and restaurants usually with outdoor seating make Xintiandi a popular shopping spot in the day and a magnet for nightlife. Merchandise is generally pricey compared to other city shopping areas, but without noisy traffic and street vendors, Xintiandi is a relaxing place to shop.

SHOPPING

Madame Mao's Dowry (207 Fumin Lu, at the corner of Julu Lu, French Concession; 021 54033551; www.madamemaosdowry.com) has a wide selection of objects from daily life such as crockery, old photographs, propaganda posters, vintage furnishings and other items that might have appealed to Mao's wife.

Number D (No. 25, Lane 181, Taicang Lu, near Huangpi Nan Lu, Xintiandi; 021 63262140; www.numberd.com) features the innovative jewelry of Shanghai designer Jiang Qiong Er, a former student of the National School of Decorative Arts in Paris. Working with diverse industrial materials, this multi-talented painter-photographer-designer markets her unique pieces to an international clientele.

🐼 Arts and Crafts

Lan Yin Hua Bu Guan (No. 24, Lane 637, Changle Lu, near Changshu Lu; open daily 9am–5pm; 021 54037947), a shop with a museum in the old French Concession, entices shoppers with such merchandise as beautiful printed papers, handmade purses, clothing, and the blue fabric of Nankin.

Shanghai Arts and Crafts Museum (see Map p46; 79 Fenyang Lu)—formerly the Arts and Crafts Research Center—is now devoted to displaying the works of the city's artisans. On the first floor, a boutique sells the crafts once made in the studios here.

Jingdezhen Yishu Ciqi (1175–1183 Nanjing Xi Lu) is a boutique specializing in the porcelain made in the city of Jingdezhen. A world capital for the manufacture

of porcelain, Jingdezhen, in the province of Jiangxi, is responsible for half of China's porcelain production.

Spin (Building 3, 758 Julu Lu, at the corner of Fumin Lu; 021 62792545) is a workshop with an outlet for the sale of the beautiful china made in Jingdezhen (see above). Spin sells the tableware to the Shanghai restaurant **Shintori** (see RESTAURANTS).

Shanghai Art Museum Store (325 Nanjing Xi Lu and in Xintiandi at 123 Taicang Lu; open daily 9am–6pm) has many handsome objects such as calligraphy brushes, porcelain wares, embroidered slippers, silks, jade jewelry, as well as reproductions of works from the museum.

Morganshan Lu (see Map p36, southeast of Mengqing Park) has been the center of Shanghai's hip arts scene since 2000. In the late 1990s, the old warehouses and vacant factory buildings along Suzhou Creek were slowly converted to studios and galleries by Shanghai's emerging artists. Among the important galleries there today are **BizArt**, which highlights the experimental work of young artists, mainly videos and installations; **Eastlink Gallery**, a pioneer of controversial avant-garde works; **l'Art Scene Warehouse**, which rotates the works of Chinese and international artists; and **ShanghArt**, with an exhibit hall called H Space, and the **Warehouse** holding contemporary works by Chinese artists.

Musical Instruments (Fenyang Lu) can be found in the many music stores of Fenyang Road, near the Conservatory of Music (see PERFORMING ARTS).

Books

Foreign Language Bookstore
(390 Fuzhou Lu, east of People's Square; open daily 9:30am–7pm; 021 23204888; www.sbt.com.cn) has thousands of foreign language titles and good maps of the city as well as books on the history of Shanghai (available in English generally).

Garden Books *(325 Changle Lu, near Shanxi Lu; open daily 10am–10pm; 021 54048728)* has a selection of books and guides on Shanghai, as well as a cafe where patrons can enjoy Italian gelato.

Shopping Malls

If your time is limited, head for one of Shanghai's many shopping malls. Here's a selection:

Plaza 66 *(see Map p46, 1266 Nanjing Xi Lu; 021 32104566; www.plaza66.com)* is a modern temple to luxury and consumption, where international brand names like Vuitton, Prada and Chanel are sought after by Shanghai's fashion-conscious females. A number of eateries are on the premises if you need a break.

High Street Loft *(283 Jianguo Xi Lu, near Jiashan Lu; www.highstreetloft.com)*, in the old French Concession, sits within a foxy multilevel conversion of a former textile mill, playing landlord to such stores as DESIGNPLUS and Yanche, with their focus on decorative household items; Cotton's Son and its namesake products; and SHAR's European and US-inspired clothing.

Raffles City *(268 Xizang Lu; www.rafflescity-shanghai.com)* is an 8-story shopping center attached to a 51-floor office tower near People's Square. It hosts nearly 60 shops dedicated to fashion alone, plus an assortment of stores specializing in electronics, household goods, books, sports, music and other merchandise. There are more than two dozen places to eat in the food court.

Shanghai Centre *(1376 Nanjing Xi Lu; open daily 10am–10pm; 021 62798610; www.shanghaicentre.com)* rises in glitzy magnificence from its massive base near Jing'an Temple. The retail/office/residential/entertainment complex boasts many international labels like Ferragamo, Miumiu and Marc Jacobs as well as a theater and the swank Portman Ritz-Carlton Hotel.

Super Brand Mall *(168 Lujiazue Lu; open daily 10am–10pm; 021 50495155; www.superbrandmall.com)* is the Pudong's 11-floor giant shopping center that tosses many well-known brand names into its store directory mix: Fila, Swatch, Benetton, Calvin Klein Jeans, Nike and Nautica, to name a few. The basement level holds a number of cafes, bakeries and coffeehouses.

Kinden Kuo/Flickr.com

– Raffles City – Eight stories of shopping

NIGHTLIFE

Though evening entertainment in Shanghai no longer rivals the Paris scene, as it once did in the 1930s, the city is slowly expanding its nighttime offerings. Bars and nightclubs open and close with rapidity, however, but venues are wide-ranging and include everything from the glamorous and trendy to the downright seedy (which we have avoided in our selections below).

Bars

Although some bars open mid-morning, most open late afternoon (5pm to 6pm) and close about 2am. Some nightspots stay open later on weekends. Several offer a happy hour, which is generally from 5pm til 8pm.

Barbarossa

231 Nanjing Xi Lu. Huangpu. (021) 63180220.

Located next door to MoCA, this Shanghai stalwart covers three floors atop a pond in People's Park. Its exotic Moroccan decor, complete with hookahs and Moorish table lanterns, draws a chic clientele for dinner and relaxing. A rooftop terrace and weekly ladies' night are added amenities.

Cloud 9

87th Floor, Grand Hyatt, Jinmao Tower, 88 Century Blvd., Pudong. (021) 50491234.

Perched atop the Jinmao Tower, one of the tallest towers in the world, the Grand Hyatt's popular bar offers dizzying panoramic **views** of the city. The ambience here is sophisticated à la Sofia Coppola's films.

Constellation Bar

86 Xinle Lu, French Concession. (021) 54040970.

This tiny, narrow space in the Former French Concession holds a Japanese-style bar, with a low-lit interior. The servers are decked out with black bow ties, and a variety of mixed drinks are available.

The Door

4th Floor, 1468 Hongqiao Lu, via Yan'an Xi Lu. (021) 62953737.

Situated west of the city's central core in the vicinity of the zoo, The Door is consistently tapped as one of Shanghai's best bars. Its antiques-filled Asian setting

Getting Your Bearings

For local listings for the city, check out **Shanghai Daily**, an English-language newspaper that features theaters, cinemas and concerts. The monthly magazine **Time Out Shanghai** is available at news agents and Shanghai visitor centers, with information on local bars, clubs and gigs. For the latest online buzz, access www.smartshanghai.com. Also consult **City Weekend** and **That's Shanghai** as well as expat publications distributed at hotels, restaurants and bars catering to Westerners.

Cloud 9

is complemented by live music, sometimes incorporating the sounds of traditional Chinese instruments. Drinks are pricey.

Jade on 36

36th Floor, Grand Tower, Pudong Shangri-La Hotel. (021) 68823636. www.shangri-la.com.

A world-class hotel, the Shangri-La has staggering views of the river and the Bund. One of several hotel lounges, this high-rise bar encases imbibers within a bright pink, **jewel-box** inspired space. It's the perfect place to relax with a cocktail to the sound of DJ music, if money is no object.

Jazz Bar at the Peace Hotel

20 Nanjing Dong Lu, at the corner of Zhongshan Dong Yi Lu. (021) 63216888. www.fairmont.com.

The famous Jazz Bar has always been the hang-out of a talented group of veteran musicians, whose selections evoke the atmosphere of the 1930s. With the renovation of the Peace Hotel, scheduled for completion in 2010, jazz lovers will have to wait to see what's in store.

Le Bar Rouge

7th Floor, Bund 18, 18 Zhongshan Dong Yi Lu. (021) 63391199. www.bar-rouge-shanghai.com.

This bar has been a lively, well-patronized entertainment spot since its opening in 2004, with regularly scheduled disco parties. The terrace has incredible views of the river and the Pudong.

M - The Glamour Bar

6th Floor, No. 5 The Bund (at Guangdong Lu). (021) 63509988 or 63293751. www.m-theglamour bar.com.

The decade-old M on the Bund Restaurant has spectacular views of the district. Its newer (2006) curved bar was patterned on a high heel. Devotees not only sip cocktails, mojitos and **martinis,** but enjoy a bar menu of items ranging from frog legs to fish pie.

Manifesto

748 Julu Lu, east of Fumin Lu, French Concession. (021) 62899108.

Accessible upstairs from within Mesa restaurant, this modern

TMSK

lounge is a sought-out spot for relaxation and conversation amid a background of DJ-spun tunes. The popular outdoor terrace, an extension of the bar, makes a great place to toast the city with a cocktail. Happy hour weekdays.

Muse at Park 97

2A Gaolan Lu, (entry via Fuxing Park) near Sinan Lu. (021) 53832328. www.museshanghai.com.cn.

For several years now, this queen of watering holes continues to appeal to expats, new generation Chinese, bohemian writers, artists and photographers, with its rather decadent atmosphere.

O'Malley's Irish Pub

42 Tao Jiang Lu, off Heng Shan Lu, French Concession. (021) 64744533. www.omalleys-shanghai.com.

Ensconced in a late-19C two-story house, O'Malley's claims to be the first of the Irish pubs in Asia. Guinness on tap, pub fare (but with a price tag), live music, a big sports screen, **pool** tables

and an outdoor beer garden keep the place hopping. Happy hour weekdays.

People 7

805 Julu Lu, near Fumin Lu in the French Concession. (021) 54040707.

A tricky entryway has yet to keep the crowds away from this popular restaurant and bar. Regulars know the secret to getting not only through the main door, but also into the bathrooms. Despite a minimalist, cement-cast interior, the seating is comfortable, the lights are low and the drink offerings are varied.

TMSK

Unit 2, Number 11, Lane 181, North Block, Xintiandi. (021) 63262227. www.tmsk.com.

This "house" of glass has to be seen by night owls to be appreciated. Colored art glass pervades the ceilings, wall art, bar facing and even the wine glasses. Patrons perch on bar stools atop pink-hued glass pedestals. TMSK

Watch Your Wallet

For your night on the town, especially if you intend to bar hop, take few valuables and protect the ones you do take from possible pickpockets by being aware of your surroundings. Watch your drinks to assure no sedative is slipped into them. Be wary of overly friendly individuals, especially those who offer to buy you a drink.

is frequented for its fusion cuisine, swank bar and live entertainment.

YY Yin and Yang's

125 Nanchang Lu, at the corner of Jianguo Lu. (021) 64312668.

This long-standing Shanghai night spot is an option for those seeking a drink or a bite to eat at any time of day or night.

Clubs

Shanghai's nightclub scene centers on crowded dance clubs, jazz venues, and karaoke establishments. Admission fees vary, and lines often form after midnight.

 Babyface

Unit 101, Shanghai Square, 138 Huaihai Lu. (021) 63756667. www. babyface.com.cn.

This 10-year veteran of the city's after-dark action draws the local masses night after night to its spacious quarters (room for 2,000 revelers). Dance til the small hours to DJ picks at this member of a fast-spreading club chain in China.

 Bonbon

2nd Floor, YunHai Tower. 1329/1331 Huaihai Lu. (0133) 21939299. www.clubonbonbon.com.

One of global Godskitchen's fold, Bonbon opened in late 2005. It has

consistently garnered top ratings from Shanghai clubbers and repeatedly snags in-demand DJs. A state-of-the-art sound system, two dance floors and five bars keep the crowds coming.

Dragon Club

156 Fenyang Lu. (021) 64332187. www.dragonclub.com.cn.

Occupying part of a substantial villa in the former French Concession, this tiny place comes alive on weekends after 3am with parties, dancing and DJs.

 JZ Club

46 Fuxing Xi Lu. (021) 64310269, www.jzclub.cn.

Opened by a couple of Chinese musicians, this jazz club hosts talented local and international performers nightly. Beautifully decorated in shades of red, the intimate space appeals to serious jazz lovers.

The Shelter

5 Yongfu Lu, near Fuxing Xi Lu , French Concession (021) 64370400.

This former bomb shelter caters to casually dressed party-goers who love to dance and drink til the early hours of the morning. The dance floor is spacious and the drinks affordable.

SPAS

In Shanghai, as in all of China, massage is viewed as an essential part of promoting one's health. Massage is available in a wide range of outlets, from bare-bones salons and even blind massage parlors to luxurious spas in upscale hotels. The cost of a one-hour session varies from 60 yuans to 1,000, depending on the establishment. Common techniques include Balinese, Shiatsu, Swedish and Thai as well as *tuina*, the traditional Chinese "push and grasp" method.

Banyan Tree Spa

3rd Floor, Bund Center, in the Westin Hotel. 88 Henan Central Road. (021) 63351888, ext. 7271 or 7272. www.banyantreespa.com.

Part of a chain with other locations in Asia and elsewhere internationally, this spa incorporates natural ingredients and traditional Chinese herbs into its body and beauty treatments. Try a **Balinese massage**, or the signature massage using a herbal pouch immersed in warm sesame oil.

CHI

6th Floor, Grand Tower, Pudong Shangri-La Hotel. 33 Fu Lu. (021) 58771503. www.shangri-la.com.

This elegant, pricey retreat in one of Shanghai's grandest hotels has private suites with spa showers, bath and steam facilities and lounges. A favored signature treatment is the 1hr and 40min Jade Journey: a foot bath and **tea bath** followed by a traditional Chinese massage using a jade stone.

Dragonfly

20 Donghu Lu, near Huaihai Lu. (021) 54050008. www.dragonfly.net.cn.

With multiple locations in Shanghai and China, Dragonfly offers Chinese massage, Japanese shiatsu, Oriental foot massage, facials, waxing and nail work in a relaxing setting at affordable prices.

CHI spa, Pudong Shangri-La

Evian Spa

2nd Floor, Three on the Bund. 3 Zhongshan Dong Yi Lu, at the corner of Guangdong Lu. (021) 63216622. www.threeonthebund.com.

This temple of luxury offers a range of massages and treatments for women at atmospheric prices. Men can get pampered treatments (haircuts, manicures and pedicures) at **Barbers by Three** in the Three on the Bund complex.

Green Massage

58 Taicang Lu, Xintiandi. (021) 53860222. Also location in Xujiahui. www.greenmassage.com.cn.

Green Massage is opening branches in Shanghai with regularity. The popular chain combines traditional Chinese methods and Japanese shiatsu with aromatherapy to reduce tension and relax muscles.

Lulu Massage Center

597 Fuxing Lu, at the corner of Shanxi Lu, French Concession. (021) 64732634.

A relaxing stop in the heart of the French Concession, this massage parlor offers body and foot massages at affordable prices. Most of the masseurs are blind, and all massages are done in one room. Hygiene and cleanliness are a priority here.

Mandara Spa

5th Floor, Marriott Hotel, 399 Nanjing Xi Lu. (021) 53594969. www.mandaraspa.com.

This posh haven in the Marriott boasts eight treatment suites and a full-service salon. An elegant setting of exposed wood beams and unpolished bricks evokes an old Shanghai house. Try the Taste of the Orient: a body polish with crushed rice grains, fragrant Chinese spices and jasmine flowers, combined with a massage using sandalwood and ginger. The Pearl of the Orient facial incorporates pearls, of course.

Ming

298 Wulumuqi Nan Lu. (021) 54652501.

Visit Ming for the handsome setting as much as for the treatments. Take the little bridge to reach the Japanese-style rooms for a foot or body massage. Silk pajamas are provided. This massage center is especially popular with women.

Old House Massage

314 Julu Lu, between Shanxi Lu and Maoming Lu. (021) 62726169.

In a refined old dwelling, experience a body or foot massage in a private room, accompanied by soothing music. It's possible to choose a combination of treatments.

Pharmacie Cai Tong De Tang

450 Nanjing Dong Lu. (021) 63221160.

This traditional pharmacy sits on three floors that have retained their old, all-wood interiors. Medical consultations are given for a handful of yuans.

SPAS

EXCURSIONS

Another great thing about Shanghai is its proximity to two ancient cities and smaller canal towns that are only an hour's drive (or ferry ride) or so away. Head southwest and you'll find Hangzhou (124mi) with its famed West Lake. Due west is Suzhou (53mi), city of renowned classical gardens. Just southeast of it are the quaint canal towns of Zhouzhuang and Tongli. A ferry ride takes you southeast to Putuoshan Island (124mi), with its sandy beaches.

For suggested dining spots and lodgings for these excursions, see RESTAURANTS and HOTELS.

🐼 HANGZHOU★★★

Sitting in the Yangtze River delta, the capital of Zhejiang Province overlooks a vast, tranquil lake backdropped by soft hills on three sides. Praised by famed 13C traveler Marco Polo, the ancient city also served as the capital of the former Southern Song dynasty (1127–1279). It sprawls outward from the shores of the most famous lake in the country: 2.5sq mi **West Lake**, which has inspired Chinese artists from time immemorial. The final stop on the prestigious **Grand Canal**, which flows south from the northern part of Beijing, this flourishing metropolis of 4 million people in turn attracts millions of Chinese and international tourists each year. Indeed, tourism plays a key role in the diverse economy of the city. By day, its green valleys mark a land known for its silk, tea and porcelain production. At dusk, lakeside diners enjoy traditional Hangzhou dishes, while lovers stroll the romantic shore.

Getting There
By Plane: Hangzhou Xiaoshan Airport, 18mi east of Hangzhou's center. (0571) 86661234 or 86662404. www.hzairport.com. **Taxi** to downtown 45min, 80–110 yuans. **Bus** 50min, every 15–30min, 6am–8pm, 20 yuans. **By Train:** Hangzhou Railway Station, (0571) 87622362. Reservations: (0571) 87829987.

West Lake at sunset

Hangzhou's History

Upon the founding of the legendary Xia dynasty by Yu the Great in 2198 BC, West Lake was still part of a bay that emptied into the Qiantang River. To deal with incessant floods, embankments were gradually introduced. Later, two poet governors of Hangzhou would give the lake its current appearance: Bai Juyi (772–846) and Su Shi (1036–1101) built two dams to the north and west to tame the river. In the 12C, under pressure from Nuzhen barbarians of the northern steppes, the rulers of the Song dynasty (960–1279) left Kaifeng, their home in the Yellow River Valley, and chose Hangzhou as their capital in 1127. Because of the influx of refugees, it became the largest city in the world. The city prospered from the export of cotton. Its port opened to the world, attracting musicians, storytellers and actors. Hangzhou became a place of intellectual fervor where new literary genres blossomed, and where emperors were also painters and poets. After the fall of the Song dynasty in 1279, the city became a summer residence of emperors and a muse to artists, hosting one of the most famous academies of fine arts in the country.

Shanghai South Station: approximately 10 trains depart daily 5am–11pm for the 2hr ride, 40–50 yuans.
To Suzhou: 15 trains depart daily for the 2–3.5hr ride, 40–80 yuans.
By Bus: (0571) 86046666. Hangzhou has four long-distance bus stations. **East Station** at Shenjiamen: to Putuoshan daily 7am–5:45pm, every 30–60min, 4hrs. Also to Shanghai (arrival next to the South Railway Station).
North Station: to Shanghai daily 5:30am–7pm, every 30min, 2.5hrs. To Suzhou: daily 6:50am–7pm, every 30min.

Getting Around

By Bus: Urban transportation of Hangzhou (0571) 86046666. Tourist bus (beginning with "Y") 3–5 yuans. Air-conditioned bus (beginning with "K") 2 yuans. Normal bus, 1 yuan.
By Boat: West Lake: five departure points: www.hz-xhyc.com.

Access to the islets: by motor boat, daily 8am–5pm. 35 yuans by normal boat, 45 yuans by ornate recreational boat. Ticket includes the trip and access to two islets. Inner North Lake by electric boat, departure next to the Broken Bridge of the Melting Snows, 30 yuans for 4 seats, 50 yuans for 6 seats. Inner West Lake cruise on electric boat, departure next to Solitary Hill, 25 yuans. Night Cruise by motor boat in summer daily 6:30pm–9pm, 45 yuans. Row boat with rower, 60 yuans per hour.
By Electric Vehicle: Electric vehicles circle around West Lake. There are 4 stations: 10 yuans between each station.
By Taxi: (0571) 28811111. Light blue cars. Charges: 10 yuans for the first 3km, then 2 yuans/km until 10km, then 3 yuans/km. Parking: 2 yuans/5min.
By Bike: Yiyoutang (0571) 86434128 or 139 05814517 (cell). 10 yuans/hr (deposit 300 yuans). This company has 30 rental

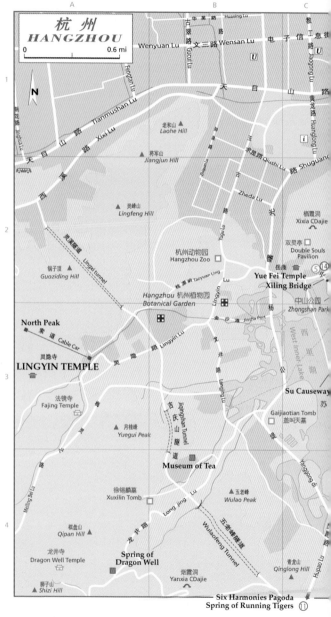

杭州
HANGZHOU

0 ——————— 0.6 mi

Wenyuan Lu 文三路 Wensan Lu 电子信

华星路 Huaxing Lu

古翠路 Gucui Lu

Fengtan Lu

Tianmushan Lu 山路

Xixi Lu

天目

山路

天目

西溪

制戈路 Zhige Lu

老和山 ▲
Laohe Hill

蒋军山 ▲
Jiangjun Hill

灵峰山 ▲
Lingfeng Hill

锅子顶 ▲
Guoziding Hill

灵峰隧道
Lingfu tunnel

天目山路 Tianmushan Lu

求是路 Qiushi Lu 路 Shuguang

Zheda Lu

古

Zhuantang

黄龙路 Huanglong Lu

交工路 Jiaogong Lu

U

i

栖霞洞
Xixia CDajie

双灵亭 □
Double Souls
Pavilion

杭州动物园
Hangzhou Zoo

桃源岭 Taoyuan Ling

杭州植物园
Hangzhou
Botanical Garden

Lingyin

Lingyin Lu

灵隐路

岳庙 會
Yue Fei Temple
Xiling Bridge

中山公园
Zhongshan Park

West Inner Lake

西里湖

North Peak
缆景道 Cable Car

灵隐寺
LINGYIN TEMPLE

法镜寺
Fajing Temple

月桂峰 ▲
Yuegui Peak

吉庆山隧道
Jiqingshan Tunnel

Jiqingshan Lu

九沙河 Jinsha Port

Su Causeway

苏

盖叫天墓
Gaijiaotian Tomb □

梅灵北路 Meiling Bei Lu

北

路

龙井路

Long Jing 路

Museum of Tea

徐锡麟墓
Xuxilin Tomb □

五老峰 ▲
Wulao Peak

五老峰隧道
Wulaofeng Tunnel

Panggong di

棋盘山 ▲
Qipan Hill

龙井寺
Dragon Well Temple

狮子山 ▲
Shizi Hill

Spring of
Dragon Well

龙井路

烟霞洞
Yanxia CDajie

青龙山 ▲
Qinglong Hill

Hupao Lu

Six Harmonies Pagoda
Spring of Running Tigers ①

104

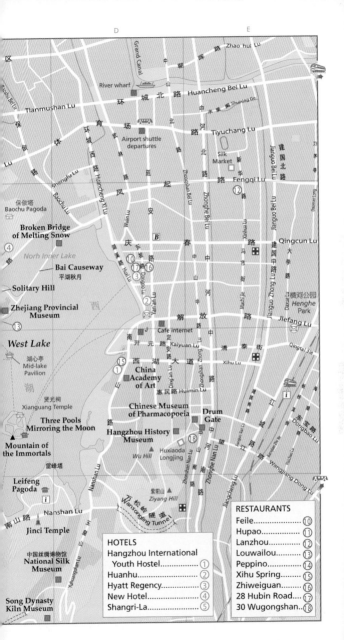

centers around West Lake. You can return your bike at any of them.

The Islands and Causeways★★★

Whether they are on its islets, causeways, bridges or shoreline, visitors and residents alike find **West Lake** truly a pleasure for the senses. Surrounded by green hills, the **site★★★** also makes room for the expanding city and its skyscrapers, but the trade-off may eventually prove too much for the bucolic landscape *(see box The Impact of Growth, p109)*.

Bai Causeway★★

About two-thirds of a mile in length, this broad, pedestrian-only causeway extending from the northern shore to West Lake's Solitary Island *(see below)* consists of a paved road, a paved promenade and wide medians. It is a popular place for biking and walking along the lake. From the mainland, the causeway begins with the **Broken Bridge of Melting Snow★**, so named

for periods when the bridge is covered with a mantle of snow: the first rays of sun melt the snow on its sunlit half, while snow remains on the other half, thus making the bridge appear broken.

Solitary Island★★

Located offshore on the northwest side of West Lake, this large, hill-shaped island offers scenic views of the lake and the city from **Zhongshan Park** *(open daily 6am–11pm summer, 8am–6pm winter)*. The favorite summer residence of Qing emperors Kangxi (1662–1722) and Qianlong (1736–1796), **Solitary Hill** offers a bird's eye **view★★** of the lake's waters, furrowed by boats and dotted with islets. From under the shelter of the pavilions, the monarchs enjoyed contemplating the lake. The island is home to the highly regarded Zhejiang Provincial Museum, part of which is housed in the former imperial palace.

Zhejiang Provincial Museum★★

25 Gushan Lu, on Solitary Island. Open Mon noon–5pm, Tue–Sun 9am–5pm. (0571) 87971177. www.zhejiangmuseum.com.

Established in 1929, this museum traces some 7,000 years of the history of one of the richest provinces in China in terms of cultural development. Among the 100,000 objects in the museum collection, the chopped **jade discs★** from the Liangzhou culture (3300–2250 BC) illustrate masterly craftsmanship, as do the **bronzes★** of the Yue Clan (Warring States period, 481–221

Zhejiang Provincial Museum

David Shen Kai/Apa Publications

3C). On the first floor are rare statues from the Southern Song dynasty (AD 1127–1279). Do not miss the **celadon gallery★★**, which displays exquisite works such as tea goblets, tea pots and flower jars, most of them from the Song dynasty.

Xiao Yingzhou Island★★

This small man-made island in the southern part of West Lake is also known as **the Lesser Island of the Mountain of the Immortals**. Following the principle of a lake within a lake, this is the largest of three contiguous islets built in the 17C from dredged materials. Four ponds are divided by four bridges joining a central islet *(see Map p105)*. During the summer, the ponds are covered with lotus flowers. The southern islet is called the **Three Pools Mirroring the Moon★**, where three miniature pagodas reflect the waters of the lake. Symbols of Hangzhou, the pagodas cast their watery reflections during autumnal nights when the moon is full.

Jinci Temple★

South of Nanshan Lu.
Open daily 7am–5pm. 10 yuans.
Leifeng Pagoda: Open daily
7:30am–9pm (5:30pm in winter).
40 yuans. (0571) 87975135.

Located east of the Su Causeway, this temple, also known as "Temple of Pure Compassion," was built in AD 954. In the 13C it welcomed the Japanese monk Dogen, who found Zen illumination under the Chinese master Rujing. Dogen introduced Zen to Japan; his Soto sect (Caodong in Chinese) is still an influential Buddhist sect today.

The main pavilion houses some beautiful examples of **ancient statuary★**, including two deities carried by an elephant and a lion. Facing the temple, the massive **Leifeng Pagoda**, founded in the 10C, was reconstructed in 2002. Escalators ascend the hill and an elevator reaches the last floors of the building, where you can enjoy one of the best views of the lake.

Su Causeway★

Nearly two miles long, this broad, pedestrian-only causeway stretches across West Lake from its northwest to its southeast shore. It consists of six arched bridges whose promenades are landscaped with silver birch and peach trees. At the south gate, the **Su Dongpo Memorial** *(open daily 8:30am–5pm)* is dedicated to the governor who ordered the causeway's construction: **Su Dongpo** (AD 1037–1101), a scholar famous for his poems, paintings and calligraphy.

Yue Fei Temple★

On the mainland, near Su Causeway. Open daily 7am–5:30pm. 25 yuans. (0571) 87996663.

A military hero of the resistance of the Southern Songs against the Jürchen invaders from what became Manchuria, General **Yue Fei** (1103–1142) never lost a battle. Yet for political reasons, he was forced to retire from the army and was imprisoned. He was charged with unfounded crimes and was killed, along with his son, under mysterious circumstances. Some 20 years later, his honor was rein-stated. His official **tomb**, shared

Laughing Buddha of Feilai Peak

with his son, was built next to Su Causeway. Facing the mausoleum, the statues of his accusers stand with their heads down. The central pavilion houses a bronze statue of the loyal fighter, as well as frescoes depicting his courage in battle.

The Hills and Valleys★★

West and south of the lake, the outlying hills and valleys are settings for cultural and natural treasures. The hills are planted with the best tea in the country; their valleys hold the secrets of silk and ceramics, and contain the mysteries of the largest Buddhist temple in southern China.

Lingyin Temple★★★

Open daily 7:30am–5pm. 35 yuans. Access to the temple additional 30 yuans. (0571) 87968665. www.lingyinsi.org. North Peak cable car: round-trip 34 yuans, up 24 yuans, down 16 yuans.

In the 4C Hui Li, a Buddhist monk from India saw this small mountain while visiting here. Legend has it that he thought it might be

Vultures Hill from his native land. He named it "The Peak that Flew Hither" or Feilai Peak, thinking it may have been moved here from India. Nearby he established a temple and monastery.

Attracting thousands of worshippers from all over Asia, the Lingyin Temple, or **Temple of the Soul's Retreat**, is the largest sanctuary in southern China. Its **main hall** is topped with three roofs and built on pillars of camphor wood. Inside rises the tallest wooden statue of a **Sitting Buddha★** (82ft high, including the base) in China. The **Hall of 500 Arhats★** holds hundreds of statues—protectors of Buddhist law—carved with expressive faces. Outside the temple, the surface, rocks and grottoes of **Feilai Peak★★★**, which is composed of limestone, have been carved with more than 300 Buddhist statues, representing five centuries of religious statuary, from the Five Dynasties period to the Yuan dynasty (13C–14C). These intricate, incredibly detailed carvings include a laughing Buddha, a sitting Guanyin, deities riding a tiger or an elephant, and a white horse carrying sutras (religious texts). From the **North Peak**★ *(access by cable car)*, at the foot of which the temple is built, a sweeping **panorama** of West Lake can be seen.

China Tea Museum★★

88 Longjing Lu, Dragon Well Village, southwest of West Lake. Open Tue–Sun 8:30am–4:30pm. (0571) 87964221. www.teamuseum.cn.

Situated in the heart of a vast tea plantation, this unique museum explores the world of tea in every aspect, from its historical appearance to the secrets of brewing it. Learn about the legendary discovery of tea by Emperor Shennong 5000 years ago, as well as about the writing of the Tea Book by "tea god" **Lu Yi** (AD 733–804). Regional variations of teahouses and other topics on tea are addressed here. Visitors can watch a demonstration of the tea ceremony.

Six Harmonies Pagoda★★

Open daily 6:30am–6:30pm. 20 yuans. Entry to the pagoda additional 10 yuans. (0571) 86591364.

The pagoda was built in the 10C on the north bank of the Qiantang River to aid navigation and to act as a safeguard against a tidal bore that could reach heights of 30ft at high tide. Sited on Yuelun Hill, the current structure was rebuilt in the 12C. Though it has 13 roofs, only 7 of its interior floors are open to the public. The galleries have retained some of their vivid original colors. Wooden balconies overlook the broad river and its traffic.

China National Silk Museum★

South of West Lake, at foot of Jade Emperor Hill. Open daily 8:30am–4:30pm. (0571) 87035150. www.chinasilkmuseum.com.

This modern museum traces the story of silk in China. On display are the first pieces found in the region dating from the Neolithic period. Exquisite examples from industrial production during the Qing dynasty (1644–1911) in Hangzhou, Suzhou and Nanjing are on view.

Well of the Dragon

Southwest of West Lake, off Longjin Lu, south of tea museum.

Upstream in the valley flows the **Well of the Dragon**, the most

---

The Impact of Growth

In recent years the landscape of Hangzhou—a metropolis of 4 million inhabitants—has changed dramatically with the rise of dozens of tall buildings and an extension of the city in general in all directions. Despite unbridled development and a massive increase in tourism (more than 40 million visitors a year), West Lake and its hills have managed to retain their bucolic air. Traffic limits, footpaths, parks, a network of tourist buses and light-electric vehicles have helped to protect its shores from degradation. Hopefully, real estate development, a constant pressure, will keep its distance from this most beautiful of China's lakes.

famous spring in the region: it gave its name to one of the most celebrated green teas in China (*longjing* in Chinese). A dragon is said to have dwelled in the spring, which according to the legend, was directly linked to the sea. The best tea plants are grown upstream on the slopes of Lion Peak. It is believed that, to be its best, longjing tea, or Dragon Well tea, should be made with the pure waters of the **Spring of the Dream of the Running Tigers★** in the neighboring valley of Daci Hill. In the 9C a monk wanted to build a temple there, but gave up the idea because it lacked water. In his dreams, a god told him that two tigers would deflect a source there. The next morning his dream had turned to reality when he saw two tigers and a spring spurting out of the ground.

Old Hangzhou (Hefang Jie)★★

The city unfolds along the eastern edge of West Lake. Nestled at the foot of **Wu Hill**, the lanes and alleyways of Old Hangzhou evoke the faded glory of the Southern Song dynasty (1127–1279). Now besieged by urbanization, the ancient city, entrenched behind the old **Drum Gate**, nevertheless retains its unhurried pace.

Museum of Chinese Pharmacopoeia★★

95 Dajing Xiang. Open daily 8:30am–4pm. 10 yuans. (0571) 87815209.

In the large **entrance hall★**, regular customers come and buy traditional medicines. Herbs, roots and medicinal mixtures are stocked in hundreds of drawers and small ornamental bottles. Inside this pharmaceutical manufacturer (dating from 1874), the museum is housed in rooms adjacent to the inner courtyard. In the first room, you will learn about the king of medicine, Sun Simiao (AD 581–682). The museum presents the fundamental principles, the manufacturing methods, with demonstrations, and the basic ingredients of Chinese medicines.

China Academy of Art★

218 Nanshan Lu. http://eng.caa.edu.cn.

Reconstructed in 2003, this esteemed academy (1928) now includes modern buildings unique

---

Where to Shop

Southern Song Dynasty Guan Kiln Museum – *Huhuangshan Lu, south of West Lake. Open Tue–Sun 8:30am–4:30pm. www.ssikiln.com.* This museum's store sells authentic reproductions of the famous **celadon** of the Southern Song dynasty, with its simple forms and characteristic crackled glaze. Prices from 400 yuans.

Xinhua Lu Silk Market – *Jiankang Xi Lu. Open daily 9am–6pm.* With hundreds of stalls, this is one of China's largest silk markets. Huge selection of fabrics in rolls or ready-made clothing such as slit dresses (*qipao*) shirts, jackets and ties. Reasonable prices.

Touring Tip

Of all Suzhou's gardens, Humble Administrator's and Master of the Nets are the most crowded with tourists. Go early in the morning *(7:30am)*, or visit other gardens. Brochures are available in English. An on-site teahouse at each garden makes for a welcome break. Some gardens are extravagantly lit at night. *The gardens are free to children under 4ft.*

to the Yangtze region; some of them evoke the style of *shikumen* (*see DISTRICTS, Former French Concession*). Offering a full range of study in the fine arts, the academy has several campuses, two of which are in Hangzhou. Open to the public, the academy's galleries showcase the country's most prestigious collections of painting, sculpture, fashion and design.

Hangzhou History Museum★

Open Fri–Wed 9am–4:30pm. (0571) 87802660.

En route to the top of Wu Hill, this museum traces the history of the city by way of a fine collection of relics, complete with explanations in English. Among the highlights are the **Kang mausoleum★** of a monarch of the Yue kingdom (904–978) whose sides are painted with flowers and mythical animals, and **Ding bronzes** carved with geometrical designs.

🐼 SUZHOU★★★

Jewel of Jiangsu Province in southern China, the city of Suzhou, threaded with canals, boasts the most beautiful **gardens** in the country—so beautiful that they listed as UNESCO World Heritage Sites. Thanks to new technologies, and the presence of large international firms, as well as tourism, this city of 800,000 flourishes today. Its markets and pedestrian alleyways retain a provincial atmosphere.

More than 2,500 years old, this ancient city was the capital of the Wu territory in the Warring States period (5C–3C BC). Its geographic location in the middle of some of the most fertile land in the country fostered large-scale rice production.

Canal in Suzhou

EXCURSIONS

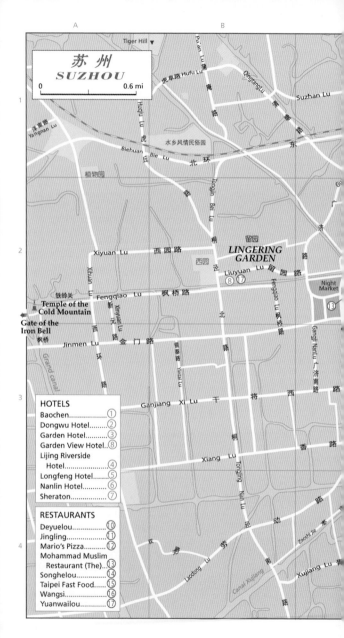

苏 州
SUZHOU

0   0.6 mi

Tiger Hill ▼

Pu'an Lu 蒲安路

Hufu Lu 虎阜路

Qingyang Lu 青旸路

Suzhan Lu

Yangnan Lu 洋南路

Hugu Lu 虎姑路

Biehuan Bie Lu 别环丘

水乡风情民俗园

北 环

植物园

Tongjin Bei Lu 桐泾北路

Xiyuan Lu 西园路

西园路

LINGERING GARDEN
留园

西园

Xihuan 西环

Liuyuan Lu 留园路
⑧ ⑰

Fengqiao Lu 枫桥路

Fengqiao Lu 枫桥路

枫桥路

Fengqiao Lu 枫桥路

Night Market

⑬

铁铃关

Temple of the Cold Mountain

Gate of the Iron Bell
枫桥

Xinyuan Lu 新元路

元和塘

Jinmen Lu 金门路

北

Gangli Nanlu 广济南路

Grand canal

西 环 路

Yintai Lu 银泰路

Ganjiang Xi Lu 干将西路

将 西 路

Xiang Lu 香

Tongjing Nan Lu 桐泾南路

Laodong Lu 劳动路

双 塔

Canal Xujiang

南

Zhizhi Jie 支硎街

Xujiang Lu 许江路

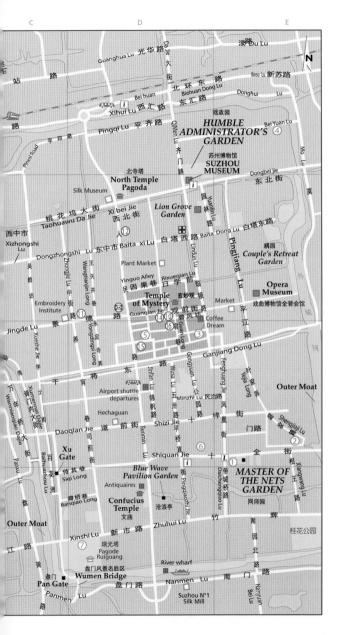

In AD 600 the construction of the Grand Canal opened Suzhou up to the markets of Northern China. A century later, mulberry trees were planted in the region, spawning a thriving silk industry. Under the Ming dynasty (1368–1644), Suzhou became a center for the arts, attracting scholars, mandarins, artists and actors. Today people still come here to enjoy its gardens, its gastronomy, opera, and other refined pleasures.

Getting There

By Plane: Pudong International Airport (Pudong), 68mi east of Suzhou; (021) 68345734 or 68346679. Departures from Suzhou every 40min, 6:20am–3pm. Departures from Pudong 10am–8pm; 1.5hrs. In Suzhou, terminal near the Guang Chang Hotel.

By Train: Suzhou Railway Station, (0512) 87622362. Regular trains from and to Shanghai 2am–midnight, departures every 30min, 1hr 10min.

Humble Administrator's Garden
©William Perry/Bigstockphoto.com

By Bus: Beizhan Bus Station, main bus station in Suzhou, east of the railway station. Departures to Shanghai 7am–6pm every 30min, 2hrs, 30 yuans.

Getting Around

By Bus: Urban transportation for Suzhou. (0512) 65637538. 1 or 2 yuans. Five tourist bus lines (begin with "Y").

By Boat: Cruise around the outer moat that circles the old town center. 1:30pm–7:30pm. 20 yuans daytime, 25 yuans at night. 75mins. 8 departure points.
Row boat with rower, 80 yuans for 40min. Departure next to the main gardens downtown.

By Taxi: (0512) 67776777, www.0512taxi.com. 10 yuans for the first 3km (1.8mi) including 5min parking, then 1.82 yuans/km. Parking: 1 yuan/5min.

By Bike: Rentals at Suzhou Railway Station and Nanlin Hotel. 7 yuans a day. You'll have to leave your passport as a security deposit.

By Rickshaw: Convenient means of transport for exploring the old town. 2–5 yuans. Make sure you agree on the price and destination with the driver beforehand.

Old Center★★★

Protected from the major arteries by the canal, Suzhou's ancient center, once enclosed with a wall, has preserved what Marco Polo called the "Venice of the Orient." Around **Pingjiang Lu**—a lane with old buildings and interesting shops that parallels the canal—as well as inside the 70 or so gardens, life moves at a different pace. Visit a garden or two for rest and refreshment, and don't miss the magnificent Suzhou Museum.

Master of the Nets Garden

Humble Administrator's Garden★★★

Open daily 7:30am–5:30pm (5pm in winter). Last admission 30min before closing. 70 yuans in summer, 50 yuans in winter. (0512) 67510286. www.szzzy.cn. Spring and autumn are best times to view the blossoms.

According to the precepts of Chinese poet Pan Yue, "to cultivate one's garden and to sell the product of one's land, such is the policy of the humble." The imperial censor Wang Xianzheng had this garden built in the 16C, far from Beijing's affairs of state. Divided into three parts around a central lake, the 13-acre garden is the largest in Suzhou, with dozens of halls and pavilions. It focuses on perspectives and the diversity of landscapes, without excessive decoration. The east section gives prominence to lawns. The west section is famous for the part of a pavilion called the **36 Ducks Mandarin Hall★**, which is built on stilts and adorned with blue stained glass. The West garden's **center★★** is the vast lake dotted with craggy, man-made islands. Linger by the **moon gates★** that offer several perspectives according to where you stand.

Master of the Nets Garden★★★

Open daily 7:30am–5:30pm (5pm in winter). Last admission 30min before closing. 30 yuans in summer, 20 yuans in winter. (0512) 65293190. www.szwsy.com.

Sitting in the southeast section of the old city, apart from the crowded main streets, this garden demonstrates Chinese virtuosity in re-creating nature in harmony with architecture and art. It has been modified and redesigned many times over its 850-year existence. Behind the magnificent **sculpted gate★**, the **center★★★** of the garden consists of structures around a pond. A narrow path winds around it between the shoreline, the rocks and the plantings. From the **Moon Comes with the Breeze Pavilion**, one can contemplate the moon while enjoying the refreshing night breezes of autumn.

Suzhou Museum★★★

Open Tue–Sun 9am–5pm.
Last admission 1hr before closing.
(0512) 67575666. www.szmuseum.
com. Restriction: Only 3,000
visitors allowed entry per day.

The Suzhou Museum, which used
to be housed in the outbuildings
of the Humble Administrator's
Garden, was designed by the
famous Chinese architect I.
M. Pei, who created the glass
pyramid of the Louvre in Paris.
Pei's family is from Suzhou. The
architecture★★★ is based on the
traditional Chinese dwelling with
a courtyard and garden, and the
result is breathtaking.
The museum is international in
scale, maintaining a collection
of some 30,000 items, including
artifacts and artworks from
the Ming and Qing dynasties.
Highlights include a miniature
pagoda★★ made of gold and
jade, as well as **relics★** from the
Wu kingdom (6C–5C BC), such as
pottery, swords and jade jewelry.
A contemporary **wing★★** houses
the works of artists Zao Wou-ki, Cai
Guoqiang and Xu Bing. Another

area is dedicated to temporary
exhibits. Your ticket provides
access to the adjacent **Prince
Zhong Mansion★**, built in 1860
and renovated a few years ago.

Blue Wave Pavilion Garden★★

Open daily 7:30am–5:30pm
(5pm in winter). Last admission
30min before closing. 20 yuans in
summer, 15 yuans in winter.
(0512) 65194375.

A quiet retreat, Suzhou's oldest
garden was built in the 11C by
the poet Shu Shunqin. It consists
of several smaller gardens with
courtyards, one whose hall is
punctuated with 108 carved
windows★★. At the top of a small
central hill rises the Blue Wave
Pavilion. The element of water is
largely absent, except for the canal
outside the grounds, which can
be seen from the **Watching Fish
Pavilion★**.

Couple's Retreat Garden★★

Open daily 7:30am–5:30pm (8am–
5pm in winter). Last admission
30min before closing. 20 yuans

Suzhou's Classical Gardens

Chinese classical gardens juxtapose man-made natural settings with
architecture and the arts. Traditionally incorporating pavilions, water
elements, rocks, hills, trees, bamboo and other plants, these re-created
settings often reflect scenes from Chinese paintings. Suzhou's first
garden was reputedly that of the emperor of the Wu territory in the
Spring and Autumn Period (770–476 BC). During the Ming (1368–1644)
and Qing (1644–1911) dynasties, aristocrats created many of Suzhou's
gardens. The Ming gardens, in particular, centered on a pond with
pavilions around it. From the 16C and to the 18C, close to 200 gardens
graced the city. Today's gardens have been altered many times from
their original states. In 1997, Suzhou's classical gardens were enscribed
as UNESCO World Heritage Sites. *For tips on visiting the gardens, see
Touring Tip p111.*

Lion Grove Garden

*in summer, 15 yuans in winter.
Crossing of the canal by row boat:
10 yuans. (0512) 67272717.*

Accessible by boat, this small garden is bordered by canals on three sides and lies at the end of a canal shaded by willow trees. Formerly the retreat of a governor and his wife, it is divided, just like a couple, into two parts, east and west, around a residential area. The pavilion called "To My Love" faces a small granite hill in the middle of the garden's east side.

Lion Grove Garden★★

Open daily 7:30am–5:30pm. Last admission 30min before closing. 30 yuans in summer, 20 yuans in winter. Crossing of the canal by row boat: 10 yuans. (0512) 67773263.

Accessible by boat, this garden, inscribed on the UNESCO World Heritage List in 2000, was built in the 14C by Zen Buddhist monks in honor of their master Tian Ru, who lived for a long time in the Lion Peak area of Hangzhou in neighboring Zhejiang Province. The **rockeries★**, some of them thought to look like lions, provide

a perspective of the main courtyard and the central pond.

Confucius Temple★

Open daily 8am–4:30pm. (0512) 65197203.

Crowned by an impressive double-eaved roof with flying corners, this 12C temple houses the **Hall of Great Achievements**, built on 50 massive pillars made of trees from the Nanmu Forest near Hangzhou. In the center of the hall is a giant picture of the revered sage, Confucius. Planted with 100-year-old ginkgo trees, the courtyard features a **stele museum★**; preserved within, the oldest of these inscribed stones date from the Southern Song dynasty (1127–1279) and are carved with maps and a genealogical table.

North Temple Pagoda★

Open daily 7:45am–6pm (5:30pm in winter). 25 yuans. (0512) 67531197.

Part of the oldest temple in Suzhou, established in AD 238, this octagonal Buddhist pagoda

EXCURSIONS

dates from the Ming dynasty. It rises eight stories and offers the best **panorama★★** of the old city, distinguished by its gray-tiled roofs and whitewashed houses.

Opera Museum★

Open daily 8:30am–4:30pm.

In a well-preserved lane in old Suzhou, the Opera Museum focuses on a Chinese tradition that is more than 600 years old: the local opera **Kunqu**, the oldest school of opera, originating with the Wu. Highlights include the collection of sumptuously embroidered **costumes★** as well as models of the stage. Regular performances are held in the theater at the rear.

Temple of Mystery

Open daily 7:30am–4:30pm. 10 yuans. www.szxmg.com/index.asp.

A favorite local gathering place, this Taoist temple is one of the largest in China. Established in the 3C on the site of the city's first palace, it retains pavilions dating from the Song dynasty, with their typical roofs. The sanctuary holds a collection of **tablets★**, one engraved with an image of the individual believed to have founded Taoism, Lao Tzu (or Lao Tse). The lateral wings housing statues of the deities of literature, health and longevity are well visited by students and the elderly.

The Outer Moat★

The moat that protected the city was part of Suzhou's massive defense network of sea and road gates, high walls and watchtowers (11C–15C). A few steep **bridges★**

still cross the main canal. A cruise reveals the splendor of it all (eight departure points, including the Pan Gate).

Pan Gate★★

Open daily 7:30am–5:30pm. 25 yuans. (0512) 65260004. www.szpmjq.com.

Positioned behind Suzhou's sea and road gates—rebuilt during the Yuan dynasty (1276–1368) to match the originals—this gate stands in the southwest corner of old Suzhou at the bend in the main canal. Its double portcullis, with granite doors, battlements armed with cannons (Qing dynasty) and single watchtower, efficiently safeguarded the city.

Outside the Walls

Lingering Garden★★★

Open daily 7:30am–5pm (4:30pm in winter). Last admission 30min before closing. 40 yuans in summer, 30 yuans in winter. Traditional music concerts in spring and fall. (0512) 65337903. www.gardenly.com.

Find the discreet entrance gate in front of a long residential alley and enter this exquisite garden. A deep emerald green, the central **pond★★**—reflecting the colors of yellow, white and red—shimmers in the sunlight. Seen from the balcony of the **Refreshing Breeze Pavilion★**, the scene is peaceful and awe-inspiring. In the west section, 100-year-old trees grow, while bamboo dominates the northern section. A walkway zigzags among the pavilions, offering an invitation to stroll.

ZHOUZHUANG★★ AND TONGLI★★

Situated within a maze of lakes and waterways, the charming **canal towns** of Zhouzhuang and Tongli offer a feast of sights and sounds. Their whitewashed dwellings, bridges, temples, and mansions of well-to-do merchants create an inviting setting in which to enjoy Kunqu opera, ride a row boat or watch the production of intricate crafts. Picturesque Zhouzhuang attracts artists, while bucolic Tongli is a refuge for strollers.

Getting There

By Bus: Zhouzhuang's long-distance bus station, less than a mile north of the old town, is accessible by taxi or rickshaw. Tongli's long-distance bus station, a third of a mile south of old town, is accessible by taxi or rickshaw. From Shanghai (Shanghai Stadium): daily departures morning only (7am–noon), return trips afternoons (until 4:30pm). 1hr 40min to Zhouzhuang, 2hrs to Tongli. 140–200 yuans.

By Taxi: You can negotiate with the taxi driver a round-trip taxi ride to Tongli, including the tolls (around 100 yuans).

By Car: A chauffeur-driven car can be rented, a bargain if you are with a group of people. Inquire at the local China International Travel Service office (www.cits.net).

Getting Around

By Bus: Zhouzhuang–Tongli, daily departures 7:30am–6:30pm every hour, 20–30min. 3.5 yuans.

By Taxi: Zhouzhuang–Tongli 50–80 yuans.

By Boat: Zhouzhuang: 20min ride. Departures and arrivals at the main canal. 80 yuans per row boat (8 persons maximum). Tongli: 25min ride. Departures and arrivals next to the Relics Museum. 60 yuans per row boat (6 person maximum).

🐼 Zhouzhuang★★

Zhouzhuang, literally translated as "the villa of M. Zhou," was named after Mr. Zhou Di, who built a Buddhist temple on the property of his former villa. The Old Town has retained all of its Ming and Qing architecture, and in particular,

Canal in Zhouzhuang

周庄
ZHOUZHUANG

0 ———— 164 ft

N

世得桥 Double Bridge 永安桥
太平桥 Taiping Bridge

北街 Jie

张厅 Zhang Residence

周庄博物馆 Zhouzhuang Museum

商业区

Canal Hougang

城隍漎

进厅 Ze House

① Hougang Jie

Fuhong Jie 福洪街

青龙桥 Qinglong Bridge

富安桥 Fuan Bridge

梯云桥 Tiyun Bridge

北市街

⑩

⑫

福洪桥 Fuhong Bridge

贞丰弄 Zhenfeng Long

棋苑 House of Treasures

蚬园弄 Xianyuan Jie

澄虚道院 Chengxu

中市街 Jie

沈厅 Shen Mansion

Xishi Jie 西市

通秀桥 Tongxiu Bridge

迷楼 Mi House

② Zhongshi

西湾 Xiwan Jie

Nanhu Jie 南湖街

Nanshi Jie 南市街

Canal Zhongshi

叶楚伧故居 Ye Chucang House

贞丰桥 Zhenfeng Bridge

三毛茶楼 Sanmao Teahouse

普庆桥 Puqing Bridge

蚬园桥 Xianyuan Bridge

隆兴桥 Longxing Bridge

全福寺 Temple of Full Happiness

HOTELS	Yeting..........①	RESTAURANTS	Fu'anlou.............⑩
	Zhen Feng		Fuhong...............⑪
	Ren Jia.......②		Shenting............⑫

its famous **double bridge★**.
*Tickets for Old Town range from 80
to 100 yuans a day, including access
to each landmark. Cashiers open
daily 8am–9pm.*

Shen Mansion★★

*Open daily 8am–7:30pm (6:30pm
in winter). Access to the 1st floor:
8am–5pm. 10 yuans.*

Constructed in 1742 by the de-
scendants of a rich local merchant,
this large residence boasts more
than 100 rooms positioned around
seven successive courtyards. The
first rooms were reserved for the
reception of guests, whereas the
family lived in the rooms at the
back. In the **old kitchen★**, you

will see the original cookware and
cooking equipment. Just under
the roof, the first floor housed the
bedrooms as well as study areas. In
one room stands a red-lacquered
canopy bed embellished with
gold. The rooms alternate along
two long lateral corridors, punctuated with two embrasures.

Chengxu Temple★

*Open daily 8am–7:30pm
(6:30pm in winter).*

Standing behind aging ochre
walls, this small Taoist temple was
built around two intimate courtyards planted with magnolia trees
and palm trees. Colorful fabrics
hang in the two main halls.

120

Zhouzhuang Museum★

Open daily 8am–7:30pm (6:30pm in winter).

Among the collections of fishing equipment and agricultural tools, Chinaware and other crafts, the museum exhibits a beautiful series of Go games as well as chess sets with ivory boxes, jade chessmen from the Ming dynasty and a painted chessboard from the Song dynasty. The last galleries are devoted to **ancient locks** unearthed in China that are more than 5,000 years old, and among the best preserved examples in the world.

Tongli★★

With its small limestone houses and docks shaded by old camphor trees, Tongli has preserved its bucolic setting. *Tickets for entry to the town are 80 yuans. Cashiers open daily 7:30am–5pm.*

Garden for Retreat and Reflection★★

Open daily 8am–5pm.

Sketched by famous 19C painter Yuan Long, the garden was built by the military commander **Ren Lanshen** (1838–88) after he was forced to retire. He had been suspected of foul play, but was reinstated three years later. At the end of the inner courtyard (around which were the domestic areas), a **moon gate★** marks the beginning of the garden, allowing a view of a vast pond. Centered on a pool, the garden courtyard can be observed from a **belvedere★** made of rocks carved out with a passageway.

Jiayin Mansion★ and Gengle Mansion★

Open daily 8am–5pm.

The Jiayin Mansion was built in 1922 in the style of the Ming dynasty. The second courtyard is adorned with sumptuous **woodwork★** carved with animals, plants, flowers and geometrical shapes. The Gengle Mansion, dating to the Ming dynasty, boasts a maze of 52 rooms. Behind it lies a **garden★** in which a 400-year-old pine tree bends over a lotus pond.

Museum of Sex★

*Open daily 8am–5pm.
20 yuans.*

Garden for Retreat and Reflection

The first of its kind in China, this museum is located behind the Garden for Retreat and Reflection. A mass of nearly everything associated with Chinese sex culture from 7000 BC to the early 20C, the collection is divided into four themes: sex in primitive societies, marriage and the condition of women, sex in daily life, and the so-called "abnormal" practices. Explanatory notes *(in English)* give the Communist interpretation of Chinese culture, even its sexuality.

🏯 PUTUOSHAN★★

Containing one of the four sacred Buddhist mountains, the little island of Putuoshan, located southeast of Shanghai in the **Zhoushan Archipelago**, fascinates pilgrims and tourists alike. Shaded by thousands of camphor trees, its temples honor Buddha and Guanyin in fervent devotions scented with incense and punctuated with the sounds of heady chants. On the southern tip of Putuoshan, a 66ft-high **statue** of the merciful goddess Guanyin has been erected. She is considered among the most revered deities in the Chinese pantheon. Legend has it that she smiled upon this heavenly land of sandy beaches, and prevented a Japanese monk from moving her statue elsewhere. Visitors may feel induced to linger in this earthly paradise as well.

Getting There

By Plane: Zhoushan Putuoshan Airport, on nearby Zhujiajian Island: (0580) 6260716, www.zs airport.com.cn. Served by China Eastern airlines, 258 Weihai Lu, Shanghai (021) 05808, www.ce-air. com. Several flights (1hr in duration) from Shanghai's Hongqiao Airport. To reach Putuoshan from Zhujiajian island airport, take a taxi to the Wugongzhi pier and a fast boat to Putuoshan (10min).

By Boat: From Shanghai: bus and fast boat, departures from 1588 Waima Lu (bus station at the foot of Nanpu Bridge), (021) 33765779 or 58281919. Departures daily at 9:30am and 10am; additional departures in summer at 9am and 2pm; return trip 12:30pm, summer 1:30pm and 2pm. 4hrs in duration. 195 yuans. Night ferry departs from Wusong harbor, (021) 56575500. Departures 8pm, return trip 3:30pm, 165–340 yuans.

Puji Temple

Getting Around

On Foot: If you have enough time, you can walk the trails that link the main attractions. It's best to buy a local tourist map.

By Bus: Putuoshan Bus Service: bus lines circle the island. Rides are priced according to the distance: from 2 to 8 yuans.

By Cable Car: To Foding Mountain, 7am–4:30pm. 30 yuans for a round-trip (6min).

Island Highlights

Puji Temple★★

Open daily 5:30am–5:30pm. 5 yuans.

Established in the 11C, the island's largest temple can be seen from afar, thanks to the **Multiple Treasures Pagoda★** (16C), which is quadrangular-shaped and adorned with bas-reliefs that depict the Buddha on each side. In the central courtyard, filled with incense, an ancient camphor tree attracts women, who kiss it to ensure fertility. In the main pavilion, the **hall★** holds the statue of Guanyin, built by the islanders and surrounded by yellow hangings. All around it stand the representations of the 32 lives of the Bodhisattva: as a scholar, as an old wise person, and other stages of life.

Fayu Temple★

Open daily 5:30am–6pm. 5 yuans.

Sheltered under camphor trees, this Buddhist temple derives its name from a tablet it preserves whose inscription was translated as: "the Buddhist doctrines are like rain and flowers falling from Paradise." In the third hall, a ball

Giant statue of Guanyin

© Andy Chang/Fotolia.com

adorned with nine dragons entwined around lotus leaves hangs in front of Guanyin's statue.

Foding Mountain★

One-hour walk to the summit.

Spurred on by the general fervor of the ascending crowds, you will reach the summit of the island after climbing 1,000 steps that are set among rocks covered with inscriptions. At the top, your reward will be a sweeping **panorama★★** of the Zhoushan Archipelago.

Temple Of Guanyin Who Refuses To Leave★

Open daily 6am–6pm. 160 yuans (including access to the temple and other monuments).

Built over the cave where the Japanese monk who carried the bronze Guanyin statue landed, the island's oldest temple illustrates, on its bas-reliefs, the legend of Guanyin who refused to let her statue be carried away from Putuoshan. It's no wonder she refused to leave, given the beauty of the **site★**. There's a jade copy of the original statue, veiled and seated.

EXCURSIONS

123

RESTAURANTS

Shanghai's multicultural dining scene offers an amazing spectrum of foods and settings. Chinese regional cuisines alone could keep visitors eating different dishes for weeks. Add to that refined Japanese offerings, robust Italian meals, casual French bistro, varied Indonesian cuisine and classic Indian fare, and it's easy to see that Shanghai has it all. For foodies, Chinese cooking classes, culinary tours and workshops are available to spice up your visit.

Prices and Amenities

The restaurants below have been selected for their ambience, location, variety of regional dishes and/or value for money.

Prices indicate the average cost of an appetizer, entrée and dessert for one person, not including beverages.

There are no added taxes. Tipping is not expected, except in hotel restaurants that often add a service charge. Restaurants are open daily (except where noted). Few accept credit cards.

The following legend indicates the price ranges for the restaurants described:

$	Under 50 yuans
$$	50 to 100 yuans
$$$	100 to 200 yuans
$$$$	Over 200 yuans

Cuisine

Chi fan le ma? [Have you eaten your rice yet?] Still in use today, this ancient greeting means "hello," and reveals the great importance the Chinese give to food. In a country of 1.3 billion people, the first priority is to eat to satisfy hunger—yet Chinese cooking is anything but a minor art. On the contrary, it is manifested in a thousand different forms and colors. A beautiful presentation and subtly aligned flavors are the paramount criteria for a successful dish. It's the embodiment of *yin* and *yang*, the harmonious blending of opposites, such as cool and warm, soft and hard, sweet and bitter, to achieve balance. Passionate about cooking, the Chinese people love to eat. China's cuisine can be divided into four major types: Beijing, Cantonese, Shanghainese and Sichuan, with many regional variations.

Rather than rice, the cuisine of **Beijing** and northeast China abounds with wheat bread, noodles and pancakes, and meat or vegetable-filled buns *(baozi)*. Also common are lamb dishes and pork-filled **dumplings** *(jiaozi)*, but Peking duck is the best-known specialty of this region *(see opposite)*. Winter brings **hot pot** *(huoguo)* meals, similar to fondue-cooked meats and vegetables. **Cantonese** dishes can be exotic, such as fox or even hedgehog stews, but the most famous Cantonese contribution is **dim sum**: bite-size specialties, such as shrimp or pork dumplings, steamed in bamboo baskets. Heavy use of white, sticky rice characterizes meals in the South: **Shanghainese** serve rice as an accompaniment to fish and shellfish like eels, snails, sea cucumbers and other marine delicacies (see hairy crabs, below). Other specialties of the Yangtze delta are crystallized lotus roots, Hangzhou's braised pork belly (dongporou) or Zhouzhuang's knuckle of ham.

In **Sichuan**, the oppressive summer heat encourages heavy use of spices such as pepper, ginger and Sichuan peppercorns. Rice noodles are often served with a fermented bean paste. Local tofu, mapo doufu, is known for its spicy heat. It is said that the people of southern China spice up their dishes because they believe that eating spicy food dispels heat from the body.

As for dog meat, which is rich in calories, it may be found in winter in the southern provinces. A relatively expensive dish, it retains some popularity among Chinese.

Must-Try Dishes

Drunken Chicken – This flavorful chicken (zuiji) is cooked and marinated in rice wine, typically from the Shaoxing region. Avoid drunken shrimp (zuixia), which is alive, and may be a health hazard.

Hairy Crabs – The city's most famous delicacy (dazhaxie) arrives in fall (Oct–Nov). Remove the gray matter from the crab and dig

Steamed dumplings
©Eneri/iStockphoto.com

out the coveted orange roe from inside the shell. It's best enjoyed with a vinegar dipping sauce.

Hundred Year Eggs – Duck eggs preserved in a mixture of straw and lime for several weeks take on a greenish, translucent appearance that is not very appealing, but these eggs (the Shanghainese call them 1,000-year-old eggs) are simply delicious. They are eaten cold, as an appetizer.

Peking Duck – The duck is flavored with ginger; brushed with a sauce made of honey, rice wine and soy sauce; and then roasted over a wood fire. It is presented whole to guests before being cut into thin slices. The meal starts with the giblets, wings and legs of the duck, served cold. Then the duck slices, with their crispy skin, are served along with small wheat pancakes, spring onions and a sweet, thick soy sauce.

Steamed Dumplings – Shanghai's most popular street food, these ravioli-like buns (xiaolongbao) are filled with pork, shrimp or beef and dipped in a vinegar sauce. Caution: the broth inside is scaldingly hot. It's best to let the dumpling cool down a bit before biting into it.

© Paylessimages/Fotolia.com
Steamed hairy crabs

The Bund

$ Sashi Yi Lu

Map p37. South of Nanjing Dong Lu, west of Jiangxi Zhong Lu and east of Central Sichuan Lu.

Enjoy Shanghainese specialties on the run for an average price of 10 yuans on this small street south of Nanjing Dong Lu. Hours are 7am until 9pm. **Street Food**.

$ Wei Zhi Du

258 Shandong Zhong Lu.

This neighborhood eatery is known to the Shanghainese for its tasty and inexpensive snacks. **Shanghainese**.

$$ Xinwang Restaurant

Map p36. 309 Hankou Lu, at the corner of Shandong Nan Lu.

The restaurant sits In a Neoclassical building (1918) that was the former headquarters of a newspaper. Chandeliers and Art Deco touches decorate the interior, which is usually jam-packed, especially at lunchtime. Other locations in the city. **Cantonese**.

$$$$ Hamilton House

Map p37. 137 Fuzhou Lu. (021) 632105086. www.hamilton house.com.cn.

This hip, retro space oozes comfort and sophistication both upstairs and down. Its resides west of the Bund and draws a well-heeled clientele, despite the lack of river views. They come for classic bistro fare superbly executed. **French**.

$$$$ Jean Georges

Map p37. 4th Floor, Three on the Bund, 3 Zhongshan Dong Yi Lu (entrance at Guangdong Lu). (021) 63217733. www.jean-georges.com.

This eponymous restaurant of the internationally renowned chef Jean Georges Vongerichten is upscale, pricey and popular. Inventive French dishes with Asian accents, a baroque decor and views of the Huangpu River make for memorable dining. **Fusion**.

$$$$ M on the Bund

Map p37. 7th Floor, 20 Guangdong Lu, at the corner of Zhongshan Dong Yi Lu. (021) 63509988. www.m-onthebund.com.

This was the first trendy address in Shanghai (1999), and trendy it remains, thanks to creator Michelle Garnaut. Its atmosphere is glamorous, its cuisine satisfying and its terrace sublime—for views of the Bund, the river and the Pudong. **Mediterranean**.

M on the Bund's terrace.

David Shen Kai/Apa Publications

MUST EAT

$$$$ New Heights

Map p37. 7th Floor, Three on the Bund, 3 Zhongshan Dong Yi Lu (entrance at Guangdong Lu). (021) 63210909. www.threeonthebund.com.

New Heights helped spur the revival of the Bund as a lively dining-entertainment hub by installing itself on the very top of a converted Art Deco building. With spectacular views of the city, its rooftop terrace draws steady crowds for lunch, dinner and after-dinner drinks. There's a popular brunch on weekends. **Western and Asian**.

People's Square

 **$$ Mei Long Zhen**

Map p36. 22 Lane, 1081 Nanjing Xi Lu, at the corner of de Jiangning Lu. (021) 62566688 or 62535353.

An institution since 1938, this restaurant sits in a courtyard a short distance from bustling Nanjing Road. Enjoy such fine dishes as the eggplant in soy sauce, the crab soup, or the shark or pork cooked twice and served with pancakes. **Sichuan**.

$$$ Barbarossa

Map p36. 231 Nanjing Xi Lu, near MoCA. (021) 63180220.

See NIGHTLIFE.
The only restaurant within People's Park is a Moroccan one. Both of its terraces are perfect for having a drink. Lunch or dinner can be enjoyed inside under the billowing ceiling tent or outside in the enchanting garden that overlooks a small lake with colorful boats. **Middle Eastern**.

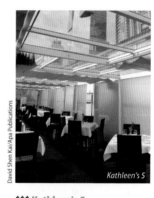

David Shen Kai/Apa Publications

Kathleen's 5

$$$ Kathleen's 5

Map p36. 5th Floor of Shanghai Art Museum, 325 Nanjing Xi Lu. (021) 63272221. www.kathleens5.com.cn.

The creation of expat Kathleen Lau, the restaurant on the top floor of the Shanghai Art Museum is modern, bright and colorful. Here you can savor a variety of meat or seafood dishes as well as vegetarian selections at lunch and dinner. Afternoon tea is also served. From the dining area, both day- and nighttime views of the People's Park are excellent. **International**.

RESTAURANTS

$$$ Wan Hao

Map p36. 39th Floor, Marriott Hotel, 399 Nanjing Xi Lu. (021) 5359 4969. www.marriott.com.

This serene, minimalist space on the 39th floor of the Marriott Hotel at Tomorrow Square offers traditional Cantonese and Shanghainese dishes. Be daring and try the braised sea cucumber or retreat to the baked soft-shelled crab, but the barbecued pork combinations are the house specialty. **Cantonese/Shanghainese**.

$$$ Xiao Nan Guo

Map p36. 214 Huanghe Lu, near Beijing Xi Lu. 400 8209777.

A member of one of Shanghai's best-known chains, this restaurant draws big crowds, so reservations are a must, at least for dinner. Traditional Shanghainese specialties on the menu include pork, pigeon and crab dishes. Try the lion's head meatballs *(shizitou)*, a famous entrée of large meatballs made from fatty pork served with crab meat and bok choy. **Shanghainese**.

Former French Concession

$ Cang Lang Ting

Map p46. 1465 Fuxing Zhong Lu, at the corner of Huaihai Lu. (021) 64372222.

This canteen owes its reputation to a clientele of diplomatic corps staffers from the half-dozen consulates in the neighborhood. The house specialty is Suzhou-style noodles. During city festivals,

the eatery features related items, such as moon cakes and New Year cakes. Menu available in English. **Shanghainese**.

$$ Bao Luo

Map p46. 271 Fumin Lu, near Changle Lu. (021) 54037239 or 62792827. www.baoluojiulou.com.

This neighborhood restaurant, wildly popular with the Shanghainese, is the successful creation of its owner, who initially sold bicycles here. He opened a restaurant in his home, but had to keep expanding due to the demand. Shanghai specialties include the red-cooked pork belly and twice-cook lamb. Menu in English. Reservations a must. **Shanghainese**.

$$$ 1931

Map p47. 112 Maoming Lu, near Nanchang Lu. (021) 64725264.

The former romantic nostalgia of this intimate space has faded, given its recent refurbishment as a Western-style eatery. The spirit of 1930s Shanghai lingers, however, in the wall art and *qipao*-attired staff. The food is good, consisting mainly of Shanghai specialties. Reservations recommended. Be alert: the sign outside is miniscule. **Shanghainese**.

$$$ Dian Shi Zhai Restaurant

Map p46. 320 Yongjia Lu, near Xiangyang Lu. (021) 54650271 or 54650270.

Sitting within a large house, simply yet tastefully restored, Dian Shi Zhai serves up reliable Shang-hainese food. Try the tofu and chopped herbs, or the mushroom dishes, which are particularly tasty. Menu in Chinese. **Shanghainese**.

$$$ Mesa-Manifesto

Map p46. 748 Julu Lu, near Fumin Lu. (021) 62899108. www.mesa-manifesto.com.

This swank restaurant and bar *(see NIGHTLIFE)* is a favorite address of Shanghai's expatriates. Its loft-like feel—à la New York—an outdoor terrace, and Australian-inspired Asian dishes are what bring them back time after time. The Sunday brunch *(11:30am–4pm)* is quite popular. **Fusion**.

$$$ People 7

Map p46. 805 Julu Lu, near Fumin Lu. (021) 54040707.

See NIGHTLIFE. The last in a Taiwanese restaurant chain (People 6 is on Yueyang Lu), People 7 is an ultra-modern bar *(first two floors)* and restaurant *(3rd floor)* that serves contemporary Chinese cuisine in a hip, low-lit, minimalist setting. There is no sign, and be sure to get the entry code when you make reservations in order to open the puzzle of a door. **Chinese**.

$$$ Yuan Yuan

Map p46. 201 Xingguo Lu, near Tai An Lu. (021) 64339123. http://en.yycy.cn.

Yuan Yuan is one of four restaurants owned by a local catering company established in 1999. The restaurant's reputation for Shanghainese cuisine is far-reaching. One of its signature dishes is braised pork with soy sauce. Some entrées combine

Mesa-Manifesto

Chinese ingredients with Japanese cuisine. **Fusion**.

$$$$ Sasha's

Map p46. 11 Dongping Lu, at the corner of Hengshan Lu. (021) 64746628. www.sashas-shanghai.com.

Another favorite rendezvous of the expat community, this handsome three-story colonial villa is home to Sasha's, known for its fusion food and spacious outdoor terrace at the rear. The often-packed bar is attended by English-speaking staff. A popular weekend brunch is served until 5pm. **Fusion**.

$$$$ Shintori

Map p46. 803 Julu Lu, near Fumin Lu. 021) 54045252. Lunch weekends only.

The entrance to this shrine of Japanese cuisine may be difficult to find, since there's no sign. But at the end of the bamboo-lined path, the restaurant is cavernous, a visionary design of concrete walls and etched glass. Even the table service is a feast for the eyes. Try the cod in miso sauce. The dessert menu is remarkable: be sure to order the green-tea tiramisu. Reservations imperative. **Japanese**.

RESTAURANTS

Afternoon Tea in Shanghai

Although afternoon tea in Shanghai is not the formal British version with crumpets and Devonshire cream, here are some pleasant places in which to enjoy a cup of Chinese tea. The celebrated **Huxinting** teahouse in Yu Garden *(see PARKS AND GARDENS)* is a must-see. **Gu Yuan Tea Art House** *(1315 Fuxing Zhong Lu at Fanyang Lu; open daily 10am–2pm; 021 64454625)* is a traditional teahouse furnished with antiques in the old French Concession. A modern take on the Chinese teahouse, **Harn Sheh** *(10 Hengshan Lu; 021 64746548)* serves health drinks and food, including many desserts; try the Pearl Barley Milk Tea. On a quiet street in the French Concession, **Old China Hand Reading Room** *(27 Shaoxing Lu, near Shanxi Nan Lu; 021 64732526; www.han-yuan.com)* is a bookstore that serves teas and coffees. **Kathleen's 5** *(see RESTAURANTS)* offers an afternoon tea *(daily 2:30pm–5pm)* with finger sandwiches and desserts.

David Shen Kai/Apa Publications

$$$$ Taiyuan Villa Restaurant

Map p46. 160 Taiyuan Lu. (021) 64338240.www.ruijinhotelsh.com. Dinner only.

See HOTELS.
Have a meal here just to see the villa itself and the beautiful grounds of this former estate. Dining rooms are richly appointed, and the food and service are what you would expect. Reservations are imperative. **Chinese**.

 $$$$ Ye Shanghai

Map p47. 338 Huangpi Nan Lu. (021) 63112323. www.elite-concepts.com.

This inviting restaurant is a sibling in a chain of upscale dining properties located in Hong Kong, Macau and Beijing. The new darling of the Xintiandi neighborhood celebrates the cooking of Shanghai and surrounding provinces in a refined and comfortable setting within a renovated *shikumen*. Hairy crabs are a house specialty in season. **Chinese**.

$$$$ Yongfoo Elite

Map p46. 200 Yongfu Lu, near Hunan Lu. (021) 54662727. www.yongfoo elite.com.

This magnificent colonial villa formerly housed the British Consulate. It has been converted into an exclusive club where guests must show their credentials to gain entrance. The interior is elegantly decorated with Chinese antiques, rich fabrics and mahogany furniture. Classical Shanghai cuisine issues forth from the kitchen, but some dishes incorporate Asian recipes, such as the chicken with apple Korean-style stirfry. Reservations essential. **Southeast Asian**.

Old Town

$ Nanxiang Mantou Dian

Map p51. 85 Yuyuan Lu, before the bridge that leads to Huxinting Teahouse. (021) 63265265.

This is the most famous place in Shanghai for *xiaolongbao*, the city's signature snack. There's often a half-hour wait in line to eat these delectable buns stuffed with meat. The best way to devour them is to pierce the dumpling, wait til the broth inside cools down and then suck the meat's juices before biting into the bun. **Shanghainese**.

The Pudong

$$$ Grand Café

Grand Hyatt Hotel, Jinmao Tower, 88 Century Ave. (021) 50491234. http://shanghai.grand.hyatt.com.

Sitting high above the city on the 54th floor of the Grand Hyatt, diners can savor à la carte

Grand Café

©Hyatt

dishes from a menu featuring either European or Shanghainese specialties. There's also a dessert buffet arrayed with sumptuous creations. This airy, contemporary-style cafe is open 24/7. **European and Shanghainese**.

Near Suzhou Creek

$$$ Creek Kitchen

Map p36. 6th Floor, Creek Art Center. 101 Chang'an Lu. (021) 63809172. www.creekart.cn.

In 2005, the Creek Art Center opened its doors in a former warehouse along Suzhou Creek. Serving dishes with an Italian flair, its elegant restaurant sits on the top floor of the center. From this elevated perch, guests have views of the river's surroundings—a former industrial area that is undergoing a full-scale revival. **Italian**.

Xujiahui

$ Xinjiang Fengwei Restaurant

Map p46. 280 Yishan Lu, off Hongqiao Lu, south of Jiaotong University. (021) 64689198.

This restaurant is run by Uyghur Muslims who are native to Xinjiang Province in northwest China.

A meal here is a boisterous occasion with music blaring, waiters singing and even dancing with customers. Mutton and chicken, potatoes and bread dominate the menu. Try the roasted or barbecued lamb, and drink the Xinjiang black beer. Reservations required. **Chinese.**

 $$$ Bali Laguna

Map p46. 189 Huashan Lu, in Jing'an Park: park entrance between Huashan and Yan'an Lu. (021) 62486970.

This restaurant sits in a big Balinese-style house beside a small lake surrounded by trees. Diners can eat inside, or outside overlooking the lake. The tranquil setting and Southeast Asian decor make for a relaxed, romantic dining experience, while one feasts on refined Indonesian cuisine. **Indonesian.**

$$$ Xian Yue Hien Restaurant

Map p46. 849 Huashan Lu, in Ding Xiang Garden. Closest major cross street is Fuxing Xi Lu. (021) 62511166.

This restaurant serves fine Cantonese cuisine, including dim sum and lion's head meatballs, as well as Shanghai classics. You'll enjoy its peaceful setting near a lake in the heart of the splendid Ding Xiang Garden. **Cantonese.**

$$$ Ye Olde Station Restaurant

Map p46. 201 Caoxi Bei Lu, Xujiahui. (021) 64272233.

Located in the vicinity of the St. Ignatius Cathedral, this kitchen specializes in traditional Shanghai cuisine. It occupies what is thought to be a former train station. You can dine in one of two rail cars in the garden: one was once part of a train reserved exclusively for the dowager empress in the Qing dynasty; the other was reserved for Sun Yat-sen's wife. **Shanghainese.**

DINING IN HANGZHOU

Restaurants are open daily (except where noted). Credit cards may not be accepted.

$ Hupao

Map p105. Hupao Lu, in Spring of the Roaring Tigers Park. (0571) 87915660. Closes at 3pm.

Isolated within the woods of the park, this restaurant has a lovely terrace under the trees. Enjoy your lunch while listening to the sounds of birds and the babbling of a brook. Local dishes are accompanied by the water from the spring. **Hangzhou.**

$ Lanzhou Lamian Guans

Map p105. 143 Xinhua Lu. (0571) 87224121.

This noodle soup restaurant sits next to the silk market. It's a good place to get a quick and inexpensive meal. From behind a smoking

> **Dining Tip**
> Similar to Shanghai's Xintiandi, Hangzhou's modern enclave of **Xihu Tiandi** (*147 Nan Shan Lu; www.xihutiandi.com*), in the southern West Lake area of the city, has an array of trendy restaurants and cafes along tree-lined streets that you might consider as a dining spot.

Dongpo pork

© Hongqi Zhang/Dreamstime.com

What is Hangzhou Cuisine?
Seafood and green vegetables dominate the menus of the restaurants in Hangzhou. Longjing tea-fried shrimp and sweet and sour lake fish are popular dishes here. Perhaps the most famous Hangzhou dish is dongpo meat, made from pork belly. Though common in other provinces, braised pork as well as beggar's chicken (cooked for a long time in lotus leaves) are much-requested entrées as well. The local cuisine is not as oily or sweet as it is in Shanghai.

pot, the chef expertly cooks fresh noodles to *al dente* perfection. The noodles are then seasoned with coriander and served with a meat of your choice. **Chinese**.

$ 30 Wugongshan

Map p105. 30 Wugong Shan.

Open from 5am to 7pm, this small tavern is known as a lair for domino players. It's somewhat hidden by the camphor trees of Wu Hill, not far from the Drum Gate. Patrons choose their fresh vegetables and fish from the menu. The selections are then shown to the customer next to the kitchen, before being cooked at the last minute. **Hangzhou**.

$$ Feile

Map p105. 7 Baifu Lu.
(0571) 87060766.

This restaurant consists of a small room decorated with wallpaper and thick curtains. Here customers can savor excellently prepared courses of delicately seasoned fish served by waitresses in traditional costumes. **Hangzhou**.

$$ Xihu Spring

Map p105. 101–2 Nanshan Lu.
(0571) 8703551 or 87085551.
Lunch only.

Located near the China Academy of Art, this restaurant is very popular with students and other young people. Behind a façade lit up with red neon lights, speedy waiters, dressed in black, serve up dim sum dishes, lotus leaves, rice dumplings and other small snacks. Customers savor the various dishes in a pleasant setting. **Cantonese**.

$$ Zhiweiguan

Map p105. 83 Renhe Lu.
(0571) 87065871.

This popular downtown eatery has a self-service area on the ground level, where customers can help themselves to soups and dumplings. Upstairs, piano music welcomes patrons who come mainly for drunken chicken, served in a broth of lime and white wine, as well as for the beef and mushroom soup. Zhiweiguan is a rare restaurant in China that lists rosé wine on the menu. **Chinese**.

$$$ 28 Hubin Road

Map p105. 28 Hubin Lu.
(0571) 87791234.

Classic dishes are prepared
and served with a twist at this
eatery: beggar's chicken must be
extracted from its lotus leaves shell
with a hammer, and the braised
pork is finely sliced in pyramidal
shapes. From the extensive
wine cellar on the premises, try
the excellent yellow wine from
the nearby city of Shaoxing.
Hangzhou.

$$$ Louwailou

Map p104. 30 Gushan Lu, on
Solitary Island. (0571) 87969023.
www.louwailou.com.cn.

Louwailou Restaurant

Chen Zhao/Flickr.com

The most famous restaurant in
Hangzhou was founded in 1848.
It is situated at the foot of Solitary
Hill in front of West Lake. Prepared
with the utmost care, culinary
specialties like braised pork and
sweet and sour lake fish issue forth
from the kitchen. The large terrace
faces the lake. **Hangzhou**.

$$$ Peppino

Map p105. In Shangri-La Hotel.
78 Beishan Lu. (0571) 87977051.
www.shangri-la.com.com.cn.
Dinner only, except Sun lunch.

This airy, warm-toned restaurant in
the Shangri-La hotel offers casual
dining nightly. Choose from a
variety of entrées such shrimp and
beef dishes, as well as brick-oven
pizzas, pastas and risottos with
a Mediterranean flair. Lunch is
served on Sunday. **Italian**.

DINING IN SUZHOU

Restaurants are open daily (except
where noted). Credit cards may
not be accepted.

$ Jingling

Map p113. Jingde Lu, just east of
the Embroidery Institute.
(0512) 65233961.

This neighborhood joint is always
packed with students, workers,
business men and other regulars.
They come to enjoy the vermicelli
soup, fried dumplings, fritters,
crepes and other staples while
seated at shared tables. **Chinese**.

$ Mohammad Muslim Restaurant

Map p112. 25 Shenxian Jie, Shi Lu.
(0512) 65580177.

This restaurant is run by members
of the Uyghur people—Muslims
who are native to Xinjiang
Province in northwest China.
Outside, the cooks prepare stuffed
bread and skewers of mutton,
chicken and beef. Inside, behind
the kitchen window, succulent
specialties that originated in
Xinjiang Province, such as pepper
noodles in a vegetable broth, are
simmered to perfection. **Chinese**.

Suzhou date cakes

The Cuisine of Suzhou

The cooking of Suzhou, somewhat sweet, is heavily dependent upon seafood, chicken and fresh vegetables. Typical dishes include squirrel-shaped Mandarin fish, watermelon chicken (chicken served in a carved-out watermelon), and soft-shelled turtle in a cream sauce. Shrimp, snails, eels and crabs are popular as main dishes. Sweets, specifically cakes and candies, figure strongly in the Suzhou diet. Cakes with pine nuts and dates are a specialty. More than 1,000 years ago, Tai Lake boat dishes were served to wealthy merchants on board vessels on Tai Lake, an early version of dinner cruises. The main ingredients come from the lake itself, such as white fish, which is usually served steamed.

$ Taipei Fast Food

Map p113. Furenfang Xiang. (0512) 65222429.

Sitting right in the middle of the karaoke quarter of Suzhou, the Taipei restaurant does a brisk business, attracting young customers especially, with its loudspeakers blasting out the music of Taiwanese pop singers. There's a wide choice of dumplings, vegetables and meats at very reasonable prices. **Taiwanese**.

$$ Mario's Pizza

Map p113. 1736 Renmin Lu, at the corner of Baita Xi Lu. (0512) 67704322.

Situated south of the North Pagoda Temple, this restaurant is run by an Italian and a Frenchman. Open 12 hours a day (10am–10pm), Mario's serves a wide selection of pizzas, pastas and other Italian dishes. Here, you'll savor good food in a setting devoted to soccer games. **Italian**.

$$ Wangshi

Map p113. 35 Taijian Long, Guanqian Jie. (0512) 65232967. www.sz-wsjj.com.

One of Suzhou's oldest restaurants, Wangshi was established in 1887. Dishes such as green pepper shrimp, sticky rice with osmanthus flowers, wild duck seasoned with medicinal herbs, and a large selection of traditional wines are served until 1pm in the afternoon and 9pm in the evening. **Suzhou**.

$$$ Yuanwailou

Map p112. 477 Liuyuan Lu. (0512) 65333756.

Crab meat, pork balls, red beans, duck stew, and pine-nut cakes are local specialties enjoyed while overlooking one of the city's famous gardens. Typical of Suzhou cooking, there's a large selection of fish and seafood (clams, crab, eels, lobster, shrimp). In summer, the terrace next to the pond is a popular dining spot. **Suzhou**.

RESTAURANTS

135

$$$$ Deyuelou

Map p113. 8/43 Taijing Long, parallel to Guanqian Jie. (0512) 65238940 or 65222230. www.deyuelou.com.

One of the city's gourmet dining addresses, this restaurant has existed for more than 400 years; it has appeared in films and on countless travel itineraries of touring companies. Cooked in the grand tradition are crab with snow eggs, braised eel, Mandarin fish, shark fin with crab meat and other notable local dishes. **Suzhou**.

$$$$ Songhelou

Map p113. 141 Guanqian Jie. (0512) 67700688.

This restaurant is, perhaps, the most famous of all Suzhou's restaurants, and one of the oldest. Here you can dine on raspberry coulis chicken, spiced bamboo shoots, stewed duck and other Suzhou classics in a modern setting that makes for a first-class gastronomic experience. **Suzhou**.

DINING IN ZHOUZHUANG

On your way to lunch or dinner, you might meet a street singer offering to sing a few local songs *(around 10 yuans for 3 songs)*.

Caramelized pork shins in Zhouzhuang

David Shen Kai/Apa Publications

$$ Fuhong

Map p120. 38 Hougang jie. (138) 62618032. Closes at 8:30pm.

This small fish restaurant boasts two great locations: one is right in front of the Fuhong Bridge, and it has a shaded terrace along the canal and a balcony upstairs. Among the dining choices are bouillon eel, carp and other fresh fish of the day. **Seafood**.

$$ Fu'anlou

Map p120. Fu'anqiao, along the Fu'an Bridge. (0512) 57215627.

At the top of the steep stairs, this "House of Rest and Tranquillity" overlooks the roofs of old Zhouzhuang. There are only three tables for a few diners, and these are suspended over the Chinese lanterns of the main canal. Local specialties include fish. **Chinese**.

$$ Shenting

Map p120. Nanshi Jie. (0512) 57211848.

This restaurant, the most famous in Zhouzhuang, is housed In two buildings on both sides of the road, and linked together by a passageway. The local house specialties include the caramelized pork shin, dumpling soup, and other time-honored dishes. **Chinese**.

DINING IN TONGLI

Restaurants are open daily, unless otherwise indicated. Some restaurants close at 8:30pm or 9pm. Credit cards are not usually accepted.

Cafes along the canal in Tongli

$ Guanyin Temple Vegetarian Restaurant

Nanshi Jie. Closes at 4:30pm.

This restaurant is situated on a large promenade at the extremity of one of Tongli's seven islets. For lunch, try the vegetable soup, and enjoy a view of the waters of Tongli Lake. **Vegetarian**.

$ Shuixiang

122 Shangyuan Jie, on a path in Gengle Garden.

Among the series of terraces next to Tongli's Gengle Garden, you'll find this restaurant, which sits on the side of a canal. Here you can enjoy white shrimp and shells and other regional specialties. **Chinese**.

$$ Shanger

Mingqing Jie. (0512) 63336988. Closes at 8:30pm.

The most renowned regional specialties are cooked with the greatest care at Shanger. Dine on the likes of sweet potato and pine nut pancakes with soy duck. There are a number of surprising starter dishes to choose as your first course. **Chinese**.

DINING IN PUTUOSHAN

Restaurants are open daily, unless otherwise indicated. Credit cards are not usually accepted.

$ Suzhai Guan

15 Pangyao Shi Dian Long, near the Temple of Universal Salvation. (0580) 6091054. Closes at 6:30pm.

This family restaurant is located on a lovely lane just near the main gate of the Temple of Universal Salvation. Here, far from the crowds, you can savor good home cooking. The robust vermicelli cabbage soup and tofu pot with black mushrooms are just some of the specialties to try. **Chinese**.

$$ Zhongshan Fandian

Fayu Lu. (0580) 6690899.

This restaurant sits at the foot of the trail that leads to the Buddha Summit. It is renowned for its fish dishes. Kept next to the entrance of the restaurant, the fish are still alive and wriggling. They are cooked to your liking in a sweet and sour sauce or soy sauce. Local specialties served include fried celery eel and chives shrimp. **Chinese**.

HOTELS

Shanghai boasts a wide range of accommodations for every budget and comfort level. New, sophisticated lodgings are popping up with increased regularity in this city, and offering ever more amenities. Luxury high-end chain hotels can be found throughout the city center, but are mainly concentrated in the Bund and People's Square (northwest corner), around Nanjing Xi Lu, and in the Pudong. More intimate hotels and charming inns dot the Former French Concession. Budget accommodations, such as hostels, can be found in the Bund and on the outskirts of the central core. The service standard in Shanghai is largely excellent, and staff in at least the international chain properties are mostly well-versed in English.

Prices and Amenities – Accommodations in Shanghai are a bit on the expensive side. Nevertheless, you may be able to obtain a discounted rate depending upon the season and the number of nights you reserve. The hotels and guesthouses described here are classified according to the price for a **double room** for one night in high season, not including surcharges. Since these prices often vary throughout the year, you are strongly advised to inquire beforehand and check rates during the period chosen for your stay. All properties accept major credit cards and offer air-conditioning unless otherwise indicated. Some have nonsmoking rooms. Most of the hotels featured in this guide provide **Internet access**, and several also have top restaurants (*see RESTAURANTS*). Expect English-speaking staff in the international chain properties and larger hotels, but in the smaller lodgings, spoken English may be spotty at best. *The following legend indicates the price ranges for the hotels described:*

$	Under 100 yuans
$$	100 to 300 yuans
$$$	300 to 500 yuans
$$$$	500 to 1,000 yuans
$$$$$	Over 1,000 yuans

Online Booking – Rack rates (published rates) provided by hotels are usually higher than website deals. Online booking is therefore often cheaper, with package deals and promotional rates discounted as much as 30 percent or more. To book a room, check the following:

Ruijin Hotel

David Shen Kai/Apa Publications

www.meet-in-shanghai.net – Shanghai's official tourism website does not have a reservation service, but it does have a comprehensive listing of hotels, categorized by type.

Search Engines – You can book hotel rooms online on the following websites:

- www.hihostels.com or www.yhachina.com/english/index.html (budget lodgings through Hosteling International)
- www.asiatravel.com
- www.hotels.com
- www.expedia.com

To see promotions at big-name **international hotels** and book online, access the following:

- www.1.hilton.com/en_US/hi/index.do
- www.starwoodhotels.com/sheraton/index.html
- www.jinjianghotels.com
- www.shangri-la.com
- www.accorhotels.com/accorhotels/index.html (for chain hotels Novotel and Sofitel).

Hotels on Maps – The hotels and guesthouses listed in this chapter are organized alphabetically by Shanghai's major districts and categorized by price. On the maps in the DISTRICTS and EXCURSIONS sections of this guide, these hotels are numbered within a green circle; a legend accompanies each map. Some hotels fall outside the perimeters of the maps in the Districts and Excursions sections, and may appear on the Shanghai city map on the inside front cover.

Honza Soukup/Flickr.com
Mingtown Hiker Youth Hostel

The Bund

 Captain Hostel

$ 100 beds
Map p37. 37 Fuzhou Lu. (021) 63235053. www.captainhostel.com.cn. There is a second location in the Pudong at 527 Laoshan Lu, near Zhangyang Lu; (021) 58365966.

This pioneer of youth hostels in Shanghai sits within steps of the Bund. Dormitories, decorated in a nautical theme, each contain between five and ten beds, or "sailor bunks" *(cash payment only)*, and are very clean. Captain Hostel also has accommodations at a higher level of comfort and at a higher rate. A private **double room**, for example, costs about 360 yuans (around $50 USD). An added perk is the terrace bar on the roof, offering views of the Huangpu River and the Pudong. On-site crafts and cooking classes are offered each week.

HOTELS

Mingtown Hiker Youth Hostel

$ 82 beds
Map p37. 450 Jiangxi Zhong Lu. (021) 63297889. www.yhachina.com.

Located within 5min of the Bund, and not far from Suzhou Creek, this hostel opened in 2006. It sits on a street that is typically Shanghainese in character, surrounded by old buildings with clothes hanging on the lines, stalls, etc. Services include Internet access, laundry facilities and bicycle rentals. There's also a restaurant, and a bar with a big-screen TV and billiards tables. A **double room** costs about 200 yuans (around $28.50 USD).

New Asia Star Longshen Inn

$$ 122 rooms
Map p37. 596 Zhongshan Dong Er Lu. (021) 63309988.

This hotel appeals to travelers on a budget because of its handy location on a small artery in the south Bund area.

Bund Riverside Hotel

$$$ 195 rooms
Map p36. 398 Beijing Dong Lu, near Shandong Nan Lu. (021) 63522888. www.thebundriversidehotel.com.

This modern, 18-story hotel rises near the Bund at the Suzhou Creek end. The rooms are spacious and well maintained; many have a waterside view. Four restaurants include a top-floor dining spot that offers Shanghainese cuisine and great views of the city.

New Asia Hotel Shanghai

$$$ 343 rooms
Map p37. 422 Tian Tong Lu. (021) 63242210.

Occupying a large building constructed in 1934 and full of character, this hotel has several benefits. It sits within a 10min walk of the Bund. Its quality-versus-price ratio is a positive one, and it offers attractive discounts on its rates. Internet access is available and there's an on-site restaurant.

View from the top floor of Broadway Mansions Hotel

Broadway Mansions Hotel

$$$$ 253 rooms
Map p37. 20 Suzhou Bei Lu. (021) 63246260. www.broadway mansions.com.

This legendary hotel is situated near the Waibaidu Bridge on the opposite side of Suzhou Creek from the Bund. It occupies a massive high-rise building dating to 1934 in the Art Deco style. Renovated rooms facing the Bund *(above the 10th floor)* have a superb view of the Huangpu and Suzhou waterways. Guest amenities include access to the hotel's three on-site restaurants, and free in-room Internet. *For more information about the hotel's illustrious history, see DISTRICTS, the Bund.*

Metropole Hotel

$$$$ 141 rooms
Map p37. 180 Jiangxi Zhong Lu, near Fuzhou Lu. (021) 63213030. www.metropolehotel-sh.com.

This historic high-rise hotel near the Bund was built in 1930 in the Art Deco style. The guest rooms are comfortable, and there's a beautiful lobby. A nostalgic atmosphere pervades the hotel's colonial bar. Internet access available. Note that rates can be negotiated.

Astor House Hotel

$$$$$ 130 rooms
Map p37. 15 Huangpu Lu. (021) 63246388. www.pujianghotel.com. The hotel may be under renovation: check that it is open for business.

Built in 1846, Astor House was the first deluxe hotel in Shanghai,

and still preserves its cachet today. At the beginning of the 20C, it hosted such illustrious guests as Albert Einstein, Charlie Chaplin, Andre Malraux and other celebrities. Sitting opposite the Bund, the hotel is located across the Waibaidu Bridge overlooking Suzhou Creek. Spacious rooms have hardwood floors and modern amenities. Breakfast is served in the ballroom. Internet access is available.

The Peace Hotel

$$$$$ 276 rooms
Map p37. 20 Nanjing Dong Lu. (021) 63216888. www.shanghaipeace hotel.com. The hotel has been under renovation since 2007; it is expected to reopen in 2010.

The Peace Hotel

Fairmont Hotel & Resorts

This landmark Art Deco building, with its distinctive pyramidal roof, has been an integral part of Shanghai's history since the beginning of the 20C: at that time it was known as the **Cathay Hotel**, and its height dominated the Bund. Divided into two wings, south and north, the hotel was built in 1906 and 1929 by promoter Victor Sassoon *(see DISTRICTS, The Bund)*. Guest quarters and common areas are expected to be luxurious after the

HOTELS

lengthy overhaul. The property will reopen as a Fairmont hotel.

The Seagull Hotel

$$$$$ 128 rooms

Map p37. 60 Huangpu Lu. (021) 63251500. www.seagull-hotel.com.

This modern, high-rise hotel faces the Bund from across Suzhou Creek, offering superb views from some of its rooms and suites. One floor is reserved for nonsmoking guests. Bedrooms and public spaces are pleasantly furnished with European decor and Asian accents. On-site restaurants, a fitness center and Internet access round out the amenities.

People's Square And Nanjing Lu

Lobby, The Langham, Yangtze Boutique, Shanghai

Courtesy of The Langham, Yangtze Boutique, Shanghai

Mingtown Etour Youth Hostel

$ 100 beds

Map p36. 55 Jiangyin Lu. (021) 63277766. www.yhachina.com.

Not far from the Shanghai Museum of Art, this hostel is installed within an old residence. It's a convenient address for budget travelers. A quiet alley adorned with sculptures and bamboo leads to the courtyard. Though somewhat small, the sleeping quarters are nicely decorated. A **double room** is offered at 250 yuans (about $35). Amenities include a cafe/bar, Internet access, laundry facilities, a movie library, ticket reservations and a helpful staff.

Jinjiang Inn - Shanghai Bund

$$ 1,490 rooms

Map p36. 33 Fujian Nan Lu. (021) 63260505. www. jinjianginns.com.

Part of a chain of hotels, this huge hotel is lacking any specific charms, but the rooms, which are located in several buildings, are functionally furnished. Situated close to the People's Square, the establishment is well positioned, and sits opposite a park.

Chun Shen Jiang Hotel

$$ 77 rooms

Map p36. 626 Nanjing Dong Lu. (021) 63515710.

Cleanliness, simplicity and comfort mark this hotel, which is ideally placed east of People's Square on the major commercial street of Nanjing Lu. It's in a great location, especially if you want to go shopping.

The Langham, Yangtze Boutique, Shanghai

$$ 96 rooms

Map p36. 740 Hankou Lu, near Yunnan Lu. (021) 60800800. http://yangtzeboutique.langham hotels.com.

This hotel, which dates to 1934, was at one time the third largest hotel in the Far East. Situated next to a church, within a few yards of People's Square, The Langham attracts largely a business clientele and others looking for a good bargain. Stylishly appointed rooms have standard amenities. A spa and fitness room are on the premises, and an on-site restaurant serves Cantonese cuisine. Discounted rates may be available for advance reservations.

YMCA Hotel

$$ 165 rooms
Map p36. 123 Xizang Lu. (021) 63261040. www.ymcahotel.com.

This hotel represents good value for money. The lowest-priced rooms are dormitory-style, but more expensive standard and even deluxe rooms are available. The YMCA property is clean, comfortable and well positioned near the People's Square, of which some of the rooms have a view. It is housed in an 11-story building that dates to 1929.

Park Hotel

$$$$ 252 rooms
Map p36. 170 Nanjing Lu. (021) 63275225. www.parkhotel.com.cn.

Poised at the edge of the People's Square, this striking Art Deco building (1934) immediately attracts the eye with its handsome brick exterior. At one time it was the tallest skyscraper in the district. The ornate lobby retains its original features, but the standard rooms were completely modernized and unfortunately have lost their former character; nevertheless, they are comfortably furnished.

Some rooms overlook the Square, which is an incredible sight, especially at night.

Sofitel Hyland

$$$$$ 401 rooms
Map p36. 505 Nanjing Dong Lu. (021) 63515888. www.sofitel.com.

Remarkably well located on a major shopping street, this member of the Sofitel group was getting a bit dated. In 2007, the common spaces and all guest rooms were renovated, and today are comfortable and well-designed. Breakfast is served on the 30th floor, which offers a panorama of the city. There's a fitness room and a business center. Rates vary widely according to the season; a 15% service fee is charged. Internet access.

JIA Shanghai

$$$$$ 56 rooms
Map p36. 931 Nanjing Xi Lu. (021) 62179000. www.jiashanghai.com.

This hip new hotel is the sister property of the JIA Hong Kong, which was designed by Philippe

JIA Boutique Hotels
Balcony suite at JIA Shanghai

Starck. The multistory 1920s building sits within steps of People's Square, and was entirely renovated to open in mid-2007 as Shanghai's hottest boutique hotel. Each spacious guest room is individually styled with contemporary furniture from top-name designers. On the roof terrace, a snazzy bar offers a panorama of the city. There's a fitness center and a restaurant on the premises. The service is incomparable.

The Portman Ritz-Carlton

$$$$$ 610 rooms
Map p36. 1376 Nanjing Xi Lu. (021) 62798888. www.ritzcarlton.com.

Built and decorated by the famous Portman architectural group, the Ritz-Carlton has symbolized Shanghai's glamorous side over the last decade. The interior features a subtle mix of modern luxury with retro Asian furnishings. In the same complex are high-end shops and galleries as well as a theater famed for its acrobatic shows *(see PERFORMING ARTS)*. Six restaurants, a swimming pool and a spa are on the premises.

Former French Concession

Education Hotel

$$$ 45 rooms
Map p46. 3 Fenyang Lu. (021) 64660500.

This modern hotel is ideally located in the Former French Concession near the Conservatory of Music *(see PERFORMING ARTS)*. Air-conditioning, an on-site restaurant, Internet access, and

rooms with a TV and shower are just a few of the amenities.

Old House Inn

$$$ 12 rooms
Map p46. No. 16, Lane 351, Huashan Lu. (021) 68486118. www.oldhouse.cn.

This charming, intimate property sits within an updated house in a quiet *lilong*. With its simple Chinese furnishings, the decor is understated elegance. Breakfast is served in the pleasant ground-floor cafe. Free Internet access.

Anting Villa

$$$$ 144 rooms
Map p46. 46 Anting Lu. (021) 64331188. www.anting villahotel.com.

On a quiet street near the Xujiahui district, this modern, multilevel "villa" is pleasantly surrounded by trees. Choose a room with a balcony or a room with a view of the garden. On-site restaurant and Internet access.

Grosvenor House-Jin Jiang Hotel

$$$$ 442 rooms
Map p47. 59 Maomingnan Lu. (021) 32189888. www.jinjianghotels.com.

The famous complex is divided into two sections: the **Jin Jiang Hotel** itself, with parquet floors and spacious guest rooms; and the **Grosvenor House**, a former 1930s luxury residence of private apartments that once accommodated heads of State. Two restaurants serve Chinese cuisine and a Western-style brasserie specializes in seafood.

MUST STAY

There's also a swimming pool. Off-season rates are often attractive.

 Hotel No. 9

$$$$ 5 rooms
Map p46. No. 9, Lane 355, Jianguo Xi Lu. (021) 64719950. No credit cards.

Its address a well-kept secret, this high-end bed and breakfast attracts its privileged guests by word-of-mouth. Without doubt, it is the most charming stay in Shanghai. Ensconced within a *lilong* opposite the Jianguo Xi Lu food market, the former 1930s residence retains a terrace and small garden. The interior is awash with statues of divinities, lanterns, Chinese contemporary art, wood and glass. Guests are made to feel at home and invited to make use of the large living room. *One- to two-week advance reservations strongly advised.*

New Westlake Club

$$$$ 20 rooms
Map p47. No. 22, Lane 133, Maoming Nan Lu. (021) 54655888. http://new-westlake.hotel.sino tour.com.

This lodging is well positioned on the major commercial street of Maoming, but within a quiet *lilong*. The decor of the charming property combines traditional and contemporary furnishings. Rooms are on the small side, but quite comfortable. A gracious staff, on-site restaurant and free Internet access are just a few of the guest amenities.

 Ruijin Hotel

$$$$ 62 rooms
Map p47. 118 Ruijin Er Lu. (021) 64725222. www.ruijinhotelsh.com.

The charm of old Shanghai can be found in these attractive former colonial villas, now transformed into a hotel complex. The historic compound is located within one of the loveliest gardens in the city. Rooms are spacious and comfortable; those in Building 1 oversee the gardens. Internet access is available. This hotel once boasted one of the most romantic bars in Shanghai called Face, but after ten years at this location, it recently closed, and is slated to open again elsewhere in the city.

*Deluxe room,
Hengshan Picardie Hotel*

Hengshan Picardie Hotel

$$$$$ 242 rooms
*Map p46. 534 Hengshan Lu.
(021) 64377050. www.hengshan
hotel.com.*

This well-located high-rise hotel sits on Hengshan Road, the "Champs Élysées of the East," opposite Hengshan and Xujiahui parks. Art Deco in style, the structure was built in 1934. Now converted to a hotel, it is furnished with taste and practicality in mind. Amenities include free in-room Internet access as well as two restaurants, a cafe and a bakery on the premises.

Lapis Casa Boutique Hotel

$$$$$ 18 rooms
*Map p47. 68 Taicang Lu. (021)
53821600. www.lapiscasahotel.com.*

Opened in 2007 by a Taiwanese contractor who already had a shop and a restaurant in Shanghai, this hotel sits at the edge of Xintiandi *(see DISTRICTS)* and exudes urban chic and refinement. Each room is decorated individually in a style reminiscent of 1930s Shanghai. Rooms 81 and 84 have a pretty view of Huaihai Park. There's a very pleasant restaurant/bar on the premises.

Okura Garden Hotel

$$$$$ 492 rooms
*Map p47. 58 Maoming Nan Lu.
(021) 64151234. www.gardenhotel
shanghai.com.*

The former **French Sports Club** *(see DISTRICTS, Former French Concession)*, where the elite played tennis, *pétanque* and other games

Okura Garden Hotel

of leisure in the 1920s, has become one of the city's most famous deluxe hotels. The superb Art Deco building has been transformed into a modern high-rise hotel, with sleek, contemporary guest rooms. Common spaces retain an air of the opulence of the past. Several restaurants serve up local cuisine as well as Western-style dishes, and there is a swimming pool on-site.

Taiyuan Villa Guesthouse

$$$$$ 19 rooms
*Map p46. 160 Taiyuan Lu.
(021) 64716688 or 64725222.
www.ruijinhotelsh.com.*

Built in 1920 for a French count, this colonial villa *(see DISTRICTS)* witnessed Shanghai's 1920s heyday and its pre-war demise. The residence has been restored to its former charm by the Ruijin Hotel group. Choose a room overlooking the lovely gardens, and take advantage of the swimming pool at the former Marshall Residence. There are dining facilities on-site. *Advance reservations strongly advised.*

88 Xintiandi

$$$$$ 53 rooms
*Map p47. 380 Huangpi Nan Lu. (021)
53838833. www.88xintiandi.com.*

This pricey deluxe hotel located
in the trendy shopping enclave
of Xintiandi combines refined
modern furnishings with Chinese
and Western accents. Art on the
walls, exquisite floral arrangements
and polished wood floors create
a highly inviting ambience.
Streamlined yet comfortable
sleeping quarters include high-
tech amenities like flat-screen TVs.
Choose a room with a view of the
tranquil man-made lake. Guests
may access a large indoor pool
and spa. An additional 15% service
charge is added to the bill.

URBN

$$$$$ 26 rooms
*Map Inside Front Cover.
183 Jiao Zhou Lu. (021) 51534600.
www.urbnhotels.com.*

Sitting at the northern edge
of the French Concession, this
sleek boutique property is part
of a Shanghai-based hotel chain.
Minimalist-styled rooms come
with platform beds, wrap-around
sofas, flat-screen TVs and walk-in
showers. Perks for guests include
an assortment of classes such as
tai chi, yoga, Chinese cooking
and Mandarin lessons, as well as
walking and biking tours.

OLD TOWN

Currently Old Town offers few
accommodations. One is housed
in a historic building.

Shanghai Classical Hotel

$$$$ 66 rooms
*Map p51. 242 Fuyou Lu, near
Luishi Lu. (021) 63111777.
www.laofandian.com.*

Situated near the Yu Garden,
this hotel resides in a fanciful
building that dates from 1875.
The historic structure re-creates
the lavish architectural style of the
Qing dynasty, but to the extent
that its appearance borders on
kitsch. Inside, the bedrooms are
comfortable, but rather plain. The
on-site restaurant specializes in the
dishes of Shanghai.

The Pudong

Novotel Atlantis

$$$$ 303 rooms
*Map Inside Front Cover.
728 Pudong Ave. (021) 50366666.
www.novotel.com.*

Rising within the Pudong's
financial district, this member
of the Novotel group offers
comfortable, modern bedrooms
with Euro-style furnishings at
affordable prices, including 80
nonsmoking rooms. There are
several on-site restaurants and
lounges, 24-hour room service, a
heated indoor pool, as well as a
sauna and Jacuzzi.

Grand Hyatt

$$$$$ 555 rooms
*Map Inside Front Cover. Jinmao
Tower, 88 Century Avenue. (021)
50491234. www.shanghai.grand.
hyatt.com.*

One of the tallest hotels in
Shanghai, the Grand Hyatt
occupies the 53rd to 87th floors

HOTELS

Executive Room, Grand Tower, Pudong Shangri-La

of the Pudong's Jinmao Tower *(see DISTRICTS, The Pudong)*. Luxurious interiors meld streamlined Art Deco touches with ultra-contemporary furnishings and features. A stunning **lobby** with high ceilings and glass windows makes for a welcoming entrance. The views from the floor-to-ceiling windows in all of the guest rooms are the biggest attraction, if Shanghai's weather cooperates. Wi-fi, a mammoth pool, the Club Oasis Spa, and the **Cloud 9** bar *(see NIGHTLIFE)* are other reasons to stay here, if money is no object.

Lobby, Grand Hyatt

©Hyatt

Pudong Shangri-La

$$$$$ 950 rooms
Map p37. 33 Fu Cheng Lu. (021) 68828888. www.shangri-la.com.

This vast hotel complex resides in two high-rise glass towers in the Pudong that offer uncomparable views of the Bund and Huangpu River. Spacious guest quarters (all have spectacular views) are equipped with high-tech gadgets like LCD TVs, fax machines and complimentary Internet. A host of hotel amenities include two indoor pools, two fitness centers, the luxurious CHI Spa *(see SPAS)*, and even an outdoor tennis court. Among the half a dozen restaurants on-site is the popular Jade on 36 *(see NIGHTLIFE)*.

The St. Regis Shanghai

$$$$$ 328 rooms
Map Inside Front Cover. 889 Dongfang Lu. (021) 50504567. www.stregis.com

Located about a mile west of the Science & Technology Museum, this posh property envelops guests in elegance and luxury. Stylish guest rooms are awash in sophistication and comfort, each with a spacious ultra-modern bathroom and views of the city. A heated lap pool, on-site spa, 24-hour fitness center, lighted tennis court and two restaurants are capped off by St. Regis' renowned personal butler service.

Near Suzhou Creek

Koala International Youth Hostel

$$ **29 rooms**
Map p37. 1447 Xikang Lu. (021) 62771370. http://yhashanghai. spaces.live.com.

Sitting near Suzhou Creek in a quiet neighborhood, this lodging lies within 20min walking distance of busy Nanjing Lu. The complex consists of compact apartments, each with a kitchenette and a small living room. They are nicely decorated, and are offered at reduced prices, though higher than typical dormitory-style hostel rates. A large **double room**, for instance, commands a rate of 240 yuans (about $35 USD); and a room with two double beds goes for 380 yuans (about $55 USD). Discounts may be available for members of International Hostelling. Guests enjoy free Internet access.

Hongkou

Nan Xin Yuan Hotel

$$$ **45 rooms**
Map Inside Front Cover. 277 Shanyin Lu. (021) 56961178 or 65400331.

This hotel is situated in a tranquil neighborhood just southeast of Lu Xun Park. Some rooms overlook

a garden courtyard decorated with Greek sculpture, lanterns and kitschy Chinese decorations. Wi-Fi is available.

STAYING IN HANGZHOU

Hangzhou is one of the hottest destinations for Chinese travelers. Book your room ahead if you decide to go there on a weekend and especially during national holidays. Lower rates are usually available during the off-seasons.

Hangzhou International Youth Hostel

$ **20 rooms**
Map p105. 101 Nanshan Lu. (0751) 87918948. www.yhachina.com.

Waiting in the garden next to the main gate, Yaya, the house dog, warmly greets newcomers. Conveniently situated near West Lake, this hostel has a quiet location. From the terrace and living room, you will be able to see the water. Dormitories have four to eight beds (hot water from 5:30am to 10:30am) and double rooms (hot water 24hrs). Library, newspapers and Internet access (5 yuans/hr).

Huanhu Hotel

$$$ **53 rooms**
Map p105. 209 Yan'an Lu near Nanshan Lu. (0751) 87062088.

Completely renovated, the Huanhu Hotel sits just 300ft from the pedestrian promenade and from the pier. The rooms are comfortable and adequately furnished.

Guest room, Hyatt Regency Hangzhou

Hyatt Regency Hangzhou

$$$$$ 390 rooms
Map p105. 28 Hubin Lu. (0751) 87791234. www.hangzhou. regency.hyatt.com.

With an indoor swimming pool right in the middle of the promenade alongside the lake, the Hyatt (2005) brings some originality to the heart of the city. The walls of the vast entrance hall are covered with woodwork and adorned with embroidered carpets. Bedrooms feature nicely designed furniture. The professional service is a plus.

The New Hotel

$$$$ 160 rooms
Map p104. 58 Beishan Lu. (0751) 87660000 or 87660008. www.thenewhotel.com.

Facing the Bai Causeway, the hotel is housed in two buildings—one a former hospital in the Neoclassical style (1922) that has kept some of its original woodwork. Early in the morning, the breakfast room is brightened by the first rays of sun rising upon the Broken Bridge of the Melting Snow. In the evening, the wide terrace on the top floor overlooks the glimmering lake waters. Rooms are spacious; some have a balcony.

Shangri-La Hotel

$$$$$ 383 rooms
Map p104. 78 Beishan Lu. (0751) 87977951. www.shangri-la.com.

Sporting a Neoclassical design with a curved roof and decorative friezes, this hotel was built in 1956 to host top-ranking members of the Chinese Communist Party. Overlooking West Lake, it sits amid old cedar trees. At the east wing's main gate are sculptures in relief. Rooms are spacious and elegantly appointed. Several restaurants and an indoor pool are on-site.

Lakeview room, Shangri-La Hotel, Hangzhou

STAYING IN SUZHOU

There are plenty of hotels in Suzhou, however keep in mind that you should reserve ahead for the summer months or national holidays. Prices are fairly expensive.

Baochen

$$ 32 rooms
Map p113. 199 Shiaquan Jie. (0512) 65307117 or 62207986.

Double rooms are comfortable and average 130 yuans in cost. Rooms are equipped with somewhat old bathtubs, however. Baochen is within walking distance of the Master of the Nets Garden. Breakfast is not available.

Dongwu Hotel

$$ 32 rooms
Map p113. Shiquan Jie, 24 Wuya Chang. (0512) 65793681 or 65193683.

At this budget lodging, a double room without a bathroom costs about 100 yuans. Breakfast is another 10 yuans. The hotel operates as a hostel, with dormitory beds for international students, and simple rooms reserved for other tourists; bathrooms are shared. A student atmosphere prevails, and there are basketball courts outside.

Garden Hotel

$$$ 161 rooms
Map p113. 477 Liuyuan Lu. (0512) 85888588. www.ywl-hotel.com.

Neighboring the Lingering Garden, this beautiful hotel is organized around several wooded courtyards. Tidy, nicely decorated rooms come equipped with a minibar, a safe and free Internet access. Guests take breakfast in a restaurant facing the main courtyard that has a garden and a pond.

Longfeng Hotel

$$ 102 rooms
Map p113. 9 Dajing Xiang. (0512) 65154101.

This downtown hotel sits at the beginning of the lively pedestrian center around the Temple of Mystery. It offers spacious and quiet rooms and various guest facilities such as a fitness room, and snooker and ping pong tables.

Lijing Riverside Hotel

$$$ 115 rooms
Map p113. 83 Beiyuan Lu. (0512) 67537777. www.szljsz.com.

This property is well located next to the Humble Administrator's Garden and is within walking distance of the old Pingjiang street and the Suzhou Museum. The Lijing includes several modern buildings, arranged around courtyards, as well as traditional houses. The rooms are comfortable and the staff friendly. Free Internet in the rooms.

Nanlin Hotel

$$$$ 210 rooms
Map p113. Shiquan Jie, 20 Gunxiu Fang. (0512) 68017888. www.nanlin.cn.

One of the highest buildings, the Nanlin boasts seven floors. Guest rooms are fully furnished with designer furniture and silks; rooms on the upper floors have

Nanlin Hotel staircase

Ben Burkland/Carolyn Cook/Flickr.com

good views. On the ground floor, the bay window of the vast lobby overlooks the garden's waterfall, designed in the shape of a hill. Note the elaborate staircase.

Sheraton

$$$$ 400 rooms
Map p113. 259 Xinshi Lu.
(0512) 65103388. www.starwood
hotels.com/sheraton.

The entry to the hotel is a high wall topped by an ornate Chinese tower; this pleasantly designed Sheraton hotel (1998) takes its inspiration from traditional Chinese military architecture. The lobby and the two main restaurants are located in the central pavilion, which looks like a pagoda. Rooms are spacious and fully furnished. There's an outdoor swimming pool with an indoor extension. Other amenities include a garden, a ballroom and tennis courts. Internet access in the rooms.

Garden View Hotel

$$$$$ 188 rooms
Map p112. Lindun Lu, 66 Luogua
Qiao. (0512) 67778888.
www.szrj-h.com.

The Garden View is located within walking distance of Guanqian Jie

and Suzhou's old neighborhoods downtown. The façade of the hotel hides a vast inner garden where bamboo grows. The hotel interior combines classical furniture with contemporary decor. There's a pleasant terrace outside.

STAYING IN ZHOUZHUANG

It's getting more and more convenient to sleep in the old towns of Zhouzhuang and Tongli. Reserve in advance, especially if you want to spend the weekend there or if you're visiting during the summer. Always ask about discounts when you book. You may find a better deal in Tongli.

Yeting

$$ 5 rooms
Zhouzhuang Map. 12 Xiwan Jie.
(0512) 57212315.

A humble boarding house on a bank, Yeting lies slightly away from the crowds. The Yang family has a few, simply furnished rooms upstairs. Three of them have a view of the roofs of poet Ye Chucan's former house. Traditional breakfasts are served in the main hall, in front of the courtyard where the laundry is hung to dry.

Zhen Feng Ren Jia

$$ 14 rooms
Zhouzhuang Map. Zhongshi Jie.
(0512) 57216036.

Facing the Sanmao teahouse, this old merchant's house has its original doors, windows and wood floors. The rooms are set around a courtyard and furnished with antiques; some have four-poster beds. Ask for a room with a view of the inner yard, rooms overlooking the street are noisy. A Chinese breakfast of rice porridge, eggs and local vegetables is served (lunch and dinner on request).

STAYING IN TONGLI

Some of the accommodations below may offer lower prices in the off-season.

Wanshun

$$ 9 rooms
177 Yuhang Jie, near Chuan Xin Lu. (0512) 63331608.

This house is attached to a church along a quiet canal next to the Yuhang Bridge. The rooms are small but comfortable. Breakfast *(8 yuans)* is served in the backyard around an old well. Internet available. Friendly reception.

Shide Hotel

$$$ 25 rooms
Mingqing Jie, first street on the right after the bridge at the beginning of the old center. (0512) 63336666.

This high-ranking hotel sits in the middle of the street of crafts shops. In the back, the rooms are positioned around two courtyards of the former residence of the Hereditary Virtues. There's a lovely dining room upstairs. Free Internet in the rooms.

STAYING IN PUTUOSHAN

If you decide to visit Putuoshan on weekends or during national holidays, make reservations in advance. A shuttle bus will wait for you at the ferry terminal to take you to your hotel (mention it when you book the room).

Jinping Hotel

$$ 87 rooms
107 Fayu Lu. (0580) 6690500.

Isolated on the road that leads to the Temple of the Rain Doctrine, this hotel is hidden behind a grove of camphor and willow trees. Opposite lies the immense and sandy One Thousand Steps Beach. Breakfast is an additional 10 yuans.

Ronglei Yard Hotel

$$ 36 rooms
In the back of the Temple of Universal Salvation (Puji). (0580) 6091262 or 6091235.

At the end of a small alley at the rear of the Temple of Universal Salvation, this hotel is a haven sitting just steps from the main landmarks of the island. The rooms are spacious, and some are more expensive. Some have a view of the nearby temple and the surrounding old roofs.
Officially, this hotel is open only to Chinese people, but you can request a room in person at the reception desk.

Citic Putuo Hotel

$$$$$ 101 rooms
22 Jin Sha. (0580) 6698222.

Facing south along the Golden Beach, the Citic has several rooms with views of the bay and the opposite islands. Breakfast is served in the courtyard. Sauna and foot massages are available. The Seashells Restaurant faces the beach and opens its terrace in summer.

SHANGHAI

INDEX

INDEX

INDEX

Photo Credits (page Icons)
Must Know
©Blackred/iStockphoto.com *Star Attractions*: 6-11
©Luckynick/Dreamstime.com *Ideas and Tours*: 12-15
©Nigel Carse/iStockphoto.com *Calendar of Events*: 16-19
©Richard Cano/iStockphoto.com *Practical Information*: 20-31
Must Sees
Shanghai Municipal Tourism Administration *Districts*: 34-57
Shanghai Municipal Tourism Administration *Places of Worship*: 58-63
©Xu Cai/Dreamstime.com *Parks and Gardens*: 64-67
©Terraxplorer/iStockphoto.com *Museums*: 68-73
©Robert Paul Van Beets/Bigstockphoto.com *Excursions*: 102-123

Must Dos
©Yurovskikh Aleksander/iStockphoto.com *For Fun*: 74-79
©Michael Walker/iStockphoto.com *For Kids*: 80-83
©Shannon Workman/Bigstockphoto.com *Performing Arts*: 84-87
©Alex Slobodkin/iStockphoto.com *Shopping*: 88-95
©Jill Chen/iStockphoto.com *Nightlife*: 96-99
©ImageDJ *Spas*: 100-101
©Marie-France Bélanger/iStockphoto.com *Restaurants*: 124-137
©Larry Roberg/iStockphoto.com *Hotels*: 138-153

INDEX